"Raising children in today's world of rapidly decaying morals and slippery values can be a treacherous journey, especially as our children become teenagers. *Parenting in the Home Stretch* gives parents a road map to keep their kids on the straight and narrow path to successful adulthood. Connie Neumann walks her talk. It's so good to read a parenting book by someone who's been there and done that—it makes navigating a whole lot easier. Connie's insight and advice is delivered with a great combination of honesty and humor, but it's not for wimps. Today's families need a good moral compass, and this book reminds us of the spiritual values we need to embody as parents so that we and our children can live in the right, full lives we are meant to have."

Cindy Grimes, editor and publisher, *Family Times* magazine

"Are your teens ready to leave home? Here's your complete nuts-and-bolts practical guide for getting them ready!"

Susan Alexander Yates, speaker and best-selling author of several books, including *31 Days of Prayer for My Teen*

"Connie Neumann does more than give advice here. This is experience talking, sharing stories from herself as a child and a parent, the experiences of others, and the good sense of experts. As they most likely read all the right books when their children were in the womb or growing in those marvelous formative years, wise parents of teens and preteens will do well to read this book!"

Eva Marie Everson, author, *Sex, Lies and the Media*

"This book will become a treasured resource you turn to again and again. It is not only a solid and practical guide to equipping children for life but is deeply rooted in biblical principles. That alone assures parenting success.

"Parenting skills like the ones Connie has shared in this book are clearly nuggets mined from the trenches. The only thing I can see that would be better than buying her book would be to ask her to raise your children."

Gaye Martin, president, Resources Unlimited

"What a great 'tongue-in-cheek' style that makes fun reading about serious stuff. Every parent and parent-to-be would benefit."

Dennis K. Baxley, Florida state representative

PARENTING
IN THE home stretch

12 WAYS to prepare your kids for life on their own

CONNIE NEUMANN

Revell
Grand Rapids, Michigan

© 2005 by Connie Neumann

Published by Fleming H. Revell
a division of Baker Publishing Group
P.O. Box 6287, Grand Rapids, MI 49516-6287

Printed in the United States of America

Library of Congress Cataloging-in-Publication Data
Neumann, Connie, 1964–
    Parenting in the home stretch : 12 ways to prepare your kids for life on their own / Connie Neumann.
        p.   cm.
    Includes bibliographical references.
    ISBN 0-8007-3079-8 (pbk.)
    1. Child rearing—Religious aspects—Christianity. I. Title.
BV4529.N48 2005
248.8′45—dc22   2005006686

For Harry, Ben, and Michele,
who bring untold joy to the journey

And for the parents everywhere striving
to do their very best

Contents

Acknowledgments

For their generous help with this project, I want to express my heartfelt appreciation to:

The gracious parents (both named and unnamed) who took the time to share their triumphs and regrets with me;

Leslie Santamaria, whose friendship and support make the writing life so much more fun;

The Johnson family for their friendship, laughter—and temporary office space;

My parents, Arthur and Marlies Blaskowski; the combined Blaskowski/Neumann clan; Cindy Grimes; the Anderson-Ferre family; Gaye Martin; Georgia Taylor; Kathy Wyatt; and my friends in VCRW and FHL for their prayers, support, encouragement—and chocolate;

Vicki Crumpton, editor extraordinaire, and the whole Revell team who caught the vision for this project; and

My husband, Harry, and our children, Ben and Michele, for supplying hugs, laughter, silence, pizza, technical know-how, and pep talks, as needed. You guys are the best.

Introduction

Not long ago, it dawned on me that my oldest child would soon be leaving our nest. One more year of high school, and *whoosh*, my baby would be off to college and the next stage of his life.

Immediate panic set in—not only because it brought me face-to-face with just how old I'm getting, but, *gulp*, how will I know if he's ready? I mean, wasn't it just yesterday that a gruff nurse marched into my hospital room and plopped a squirming little bundle in my arms with the stern admonition to "take good care of him"?

Before I could call her back and tell her I didn't know what that meant, exactly, she'd spun on her Reeboks and left. My hands were clammy as I checked inside the blanket and quickly felt all around for the instruction manual. There wasn't one! I swallowed hard and thought, *Lord, you're going to have to help me out here, because I don't know how to operate a baby.*

Some women take to motherhood like ducks to water. I was not one of them. I'd never done much babysitting as a teen (I had calculated that I could make more per hour as a telemarketer), so my experience with newborns was pretty much limited to smiling at them at the grocery store. Suddenly there I was, completely responsible for this brand-new person. It was terrifying.

I'm happy to say that with the help of both grandmas, who graciously provided a crash course in motherhood 101, I got through those first few weeks. I even learned to bathe this little person without him squirting out of my hands like a wayward bar of soap—though there were some close calls.

But we made it. At least, that's what they tell me. I honestly don't remember either of my children's first three months, except as a fuzzy mist I wandered through, mumbling, "Sleep. I need sleep."

After they started sleeping, I started sleeping, and life became much more manageable—meaning I quit barking at everyone. But as the sleep-deprived haze cleared, that same sense of panic clicked in. "Now what?" I had this constant, nagging feeling that there were instructions or guidelines out there somewhere; I just hadn't found them yet. (Although Susan Alexander Yates's book *And Then I Had Kids* was a lifesaver.)

I attended mother-type meetings and shuddered to learn some moms had elaborate charts of the various things they were teaching their children every week—charts that were color coded and decorated with little stars—while I was home thinking, *Well, we can play with clay and color in the new coloring book.*

Then things got even trickier. Way before I thought he should, Ben figured out how to climb out of his crib. Before the sun peeked over the horizon, I'd jerk awake to find him by my side of the bed—never his father's—whispering, "What are we gonna do today, huh, Mom? What are we gonna do?"

By that time I knew simply plopping him in front of the TV wasn't enough, but how do you keep a toddler busy on the twenty-third straight day of rain? (We were living in Washington state then, where people don't age; they rust.)

My mother, bless her, suggested craft projects, which would have been fine, except that when God gave out the craft gene, he skipped me. Still, I tried. We cut and pasted and glued for hours . . . days . . . eons. But sure as shooting, here came the dreaded question: "So what are we gonna do now, Mommy?" I was ready to tell Ben just how long we'd been crafting when I glanced at my watch and my heart sank. Exactly twelve minutes had passed since the last time he asked that question.

Recently, I mentally fast-forwarded to one year from now and pictured my tall, handsome son driving off in his 1972 beetle-bug to face the world. Just before he pulled away, he asked, "What am I gonna do now, Mom, huh?"

With that image spinning in my mind, I hit my knees and begged God for wisdom. The truth slowly dawned, and it was sobering. How well either of my children does when they get out on their own is directly related to how well we prepare them now. From the time our children are born, our job as parents is to prepare them for lives of their own, away from us. One of the realities of raising children is that by the time you've become an expert at it, you're out of a job.

So how will we know if we've succeeded in laying the groundwork? How can we make sure the foundation we've built is solid? A research junkie and perpetual list maker, I headed for the bookstore to find answers to these questions. I wanted checklists, benchmarks, tools; some tangible way to see if we'd covered all the important stuff.

I know my job as a parent doesn't end when my children move into their next phase of life, but I want to send them off into the world with wings AND roots—the confidence to soar and a solid foundation on which to land if things get stormy and uncertain. When the bookstore didn't yield what I was looking for—though there are thousands of great parenting books out there—the idea for *Parenting in the Home Stretch* was born. I wanted to give myself and other parents a way to measure if our kids are ready. I wanted a way to see what we still need to do and what areas we've already covered.

I don't have all the answers, but I hope these suggestions will help you prepare your children to step out into the adventure of life with confidence and wisdom. I've included stories from parents who've been-there-done-that and lived to tell the tale. I hope their stories will remind you that you are not alone. Others have walked this path before you.

Ask yourself the questions at the end of each chapter, and give yourself a pat on the back for all the areas you've already covered. And for those areas that still need a bit of work, there are resources from experts for further study.

They say that if you aim at nothing, you'll hit it every time. Though it is easy to get caught up in the day-to-day aspects of parenting, let's not lose sight of the goal: raising strong, confident, godly children. Let's be intentional in our parenting, so that we can look back on these years and say we've done our very best.

> Train a child in the way he should go, and when he is old he will not turn from it.
>
> Proverbs 22:6

1

Dealing with Authority

We have a new family member living in our house. This came as a surprise to my husband and me, since we've been through neither a pregnancy nor an adoption in the recent past. Yet whenever something goes awry and we attempt to find out how it happened, our children immediately identify the culprit. Without a moment's hesitation, the blame lands squarely at the feet of the new kid, *Not Me*.

Not Me is a busy rascal, apparently, since he is the one who drinks the last of the milk seconds before anyone else reaches the kitchen, eats the last piece of pie, and carefully puts the empty ice cream carton back in the freezer before the adults can snag so much as a spoonful. He's also the one who forgets to restock the toilet paper, hang up wet towels, feed the dog, turn off lights and appliances, and take out the trash.

Not Me wanders around our house doing as he pleases, ignoring all the rules, and blatantly tossing our authority in our faces. We're not sure where he came from, but if we ever get our hands on him—and his equally sneaky cousin *I Don't Know*—both of them are in big trouble.

On second thought, maybe we do know where he came from. It seems *Not Me* has been around since the Garden of Eden when Adam and Eve ate the forbidden fruit and then tried to pass the blame off on someone else. Of course, the problem all started when they disobeyed God to begin with. He told them they could do anything—except one thing. Naturally, they immediately did that one thing.

Who's in Charge Here?

But aren't we all like *Not Me*? We don't want to submit to authority, and we don't want to take responsibility. As parents, we do our children a great disservice if we don't teach them to obey us. It is absolutely critical that our children learn to submit to our authority. Dr. James Dobson, in *The Strong-Willed Child*, says, "The way he [the child] sees his parents' leadership sets the tone for his eventual relationships with his teachers, school principal, police, neighbors, and employers."[1] If our children don't learn to obey us, how will they learn to obey God? If they don't follow our directives, how will they learn to respect their teachers or submit to their bosses? Who will teach them this, if we don't?

The Bible has many things to say about this issue, including this: "Children, obey your parents in the Lord, for this is right" (Eph. 6:1). There is a reason this is a command and not a request. If it were optional, nobody would do it. I hated that verse as a child, mumbling and grumbling whenever I had to recite it.

That instinctive rebellion against authority is inborn, regardless of contemporary teaching to the contrary. Too many of today's child-rearing experts assert that children are born good; misbehavior is a learned response. Nonsense. People are by nature wicked—else why would we need a Savior?

If you're still not sure about this, think back to the first time your toddler looked you in the eye and said, "NO!" or threw a tantrum in the grocery store. I have a vivid memory of my toddler screaming and kicking on the floor of the frozen-food aisle while no less than five church ladies circled around waiting to see how I'd react. I did what any desperate parent would do—I scooped him off the floor, took him home, and came back for my groceries later. Alone.

Our job as parents is to help our children accept our authority and leadership in their lives. We have to be careful, though, because sometimes what we mean and what they hear aren't the same things at all. Popular speaker Gaye Martin, who raised two of her grandchildren, tells this story.

"When one of them was a little thing, she often asked to take a snack into her bedroom to enjoy. I agreed that it was OK as long as she didn't leave candy wrappers, gum, or crumbs in the bed she slept in, which was a big white metal daybed with brass balls on the bedposts. She was neat as a pin, even as a little child, and I often bragged about her tidiness when she ate in her room. She just beamed when I cast that spotlight of praise. I was so proud of her.

"After they moved back with their family in their early teen years, I decided it was time to clean the carpet and arrange her old bedroom into a guest room. When I moved the daybed, I found two big brown spots on the carpet. Upon closer inspection, I found that while she lived with us, she had been disposing of Popsicle wrappers, gum wrappers, and various debris down the bedpost.

"I immediately called her and asked what in the world she had been thinking. Her reply was, 'I didn't think you would mind if you couldn't see it.'

"I took that opportunity to explain that when in Nanie's home we adhere to Nanie's definition of clean. And the same is true in our Christian walk . . . the world will tell us any old way will do, but we are God's house, and in his house we adhere to his definition of clean."

If my husband and I had a nickel for every time we've had to remind our kids that right now we make the rules and "define clean," funding their college education would not be a problem. We tell them that someday they'll be in charge of their lives, but it's not someday yet.

Friend or Parent?

One of the common misconceptions today is that parents should be their children's best friends. Not so. Yes, we should communicate with our children; we should love them and laugh with them, play with them and talk with them. But our role and theirs are completely different. Our position in the family hierarchy is not on the same level as theirs.

In *John Rosemond's Six-Point Plan for Raising Happy, Healthy Children*, Rosemond says that families are "benevolent dictatorships" where the parents make decisions in their children's best interests. By this he doesn't mean bossing kids around for the sake of it or as part of a power trip, but a careful balance of both love and authority. Parents invite discussion—especially as the children mature—but everyone understands that the final decision rests with the grown-ups.[2]

Sometimes that means letting children reach the right conclusion within the limits of parental control. Mrs. Georgia Taylor, who raised forty-nine children—several of her own, plus dozens of foster children—told this story of how she and her husband handled one son's resistance to starting school.

"When Tommy heard that he would have to go to school, he told us he wasn't going. When it got close to the time he'd have to go, he said if he had to go to school, he was running away. So we said, 'OK. But you'd better pack a few things to take with you.'

"He went into his room and got some of his things together. Then he said he was ready to go, but my husband stopped him and said, 'Well, wait a minute. You'll probably need some money.' So Ken gave him a dollar, and Tommy put it in his pocket.

"Then Tommy thought about it awhile and said, 'I might get hungry, so maybe I'll wait until after dinner.' We told him we thought that was a fine idea.

"After we finished supper, Ken told him he'd better get going, because it was going to get dark soon. Tommy looked outside and then looked at Ken. Finally he said, 'Maybe I'd just better stay here.' And that was the last we heard about him not wanting to go to school."

Do You Mean It?

Like anyone else, kids want to know the limits. How far can they push the line their parents have drawn in the sand? My daughter was about three years old when she first questioned my authority point-blank. She was doing something she shouldn't, and I told her she'd better stop right then. She cocked her head and asked, quite seriously, "What happens if I don't?" She wanted to know if the consequences were bad enough to change her behavior. I assured her she would not be a happy camper if she did it again. Her eyes got real big, and she slowly backed away from temptation.

In her book *Mothers and Sons*, therapist Jean Lush says that a mother must set up structure for her little boy. (This practical wisdom applies equally well to girls.) According to Lush, "The *structure* must have *limits*, and the *limits* must be backed by *control*."[3]

My mother never read Lush's book—it hadn't been written then—but she understood this principle. One day when I was about twelve, Mom had to remind me just exactly where the limits were and who was in charge.

That day, I had mouthed off to Mom for some reason that made perfect sense at the time, so she sent me to stand in the corner. Not slouch, sit, or lean in the corner, but stand straight up, nose pressed directly in the corner—until I was ready to apologize.

After thirty minutes went by and my eyes were starting to cross, she asked, "Ready to apologize?"

"I didn't do anything wrong," I mumbled.

"OK, stand there then." And she walked away.

Another thirty minutes passed, and she asked again. Same response.

Friends came to the door, and eventually my legs went numb, but I wasn't giving in. I hadn't done anything wrong, so I wasn't going to apologize. After FOUR hours went by, I finally decided standing there any more wasn't worth it, so I gave in and apologized.

I learned a valuable lesson that day. I realized that my mother meant what she said. She set limits, and she backed them by control.

Today, when I see my own children's stubbornness, I am reminded that they come by that trait honestly.

As parents, there are certain battles that we MUST win. Sometimes, you just know that if you back down right then, you'll lose your authority.

We ran into a situation like that when one of our children was in middle school. Our child had plans to attend a particular party, but attitude toward me—and a blatant flaunting of my authority—put that privilege in serious jeopardy. I gave a warning and a time-out to help my offspring regain control, but the child chose to ignore the second chance and continued with the misbehavior. When I said the party plans were now canceled, instant pleading, tears, quick apologies, and major begging ensued. I held firm. More begging. I walked away. The child followed. I repeated my position and said the discussion was over.

The child didn't give up. For three days, from the time that child got off the bus until my husband returned from work, there were tears and pleading. (Kids always know the weakest link in the parental authority chain and will exploit that if you let them.) I knew we had to stand firm, so I turned a deaf ear. If I backed down, I knew we'd be playing out this same scene over and over and over again.

My worst moment came on day three. I tried to walk away; the child followed. I closed the bedroom door; the child pleaded through the panels. I finally locked myself in the bathroom with the phone, called my husband at work, and said, "Tell me I'm doing the right thing."

He said, "You're definitely doing the right thing. Hang in there, Baby, because we've got to win this one. This child has to understand that begging won't work, disrespect will not be rewarded, and we are still in charge."

I walked out with renewed conviction and informed our beloved child that if I heard one more word about this issue, the consequences would get worse. That was the end of it. And we never played out another scene like that—at least not with that child.

Discipline as Teaching Tool

Psychologist John Rosemond says that kids obey when parents *expect* them to obey. Too many parents hope their children will obey or wish they'd obey. Frankly, neither approach works. According to Rosemond, when you get sucked into answering cries of "Why?" or "Why not?" you no longer expect obedience, you are wishing for it.[4]

Depending on the ages of our children and the circumstances, we can give an explanation for our decisions. However, we should avoid getting sucked into pointless discussions and/or arguments. In his book *The Strong-Willed Child*, Dr. James Dobson says that "one of the most common mistakes of parenthood is to be drawn into verbal battles with our children which leave us exhausted but without strategic advantage."[5] The key in these situations is to realize that our children aren't really looking for information; they're trying to change our minds to get what they want.

For a while, we found that our kids would ask a question, we'd answer it, and if the answer was no, ten minutes later, they'd ask the same question again. It finally dawned on us that they were hoping they'd eventually get a different answer. My husband finally stopped this merry-go-round. When the same question was asked again, he'd simply say, "Asked. And answered," and walk away. The kids didn't like it, but they realized that cajoling and pleading and trying to wear us down were not going to gain them their goal.

We have also found that we have to be very clear in outlining exactly what we mean when we ask our kids to do something. We used to say things like, "How about getting the dishwasher emptied before dinner?" When dinnertime rolled around and the clean dishes were still right where they were before, we'd ask why the job wasn't done.

The kids would respond, "You didn't tell us we had to. We weren't sure if it was a suggestion or a command."

Big lightbulbs went on in our parental heads, and we realized we must be specific in what we say. Now we leave no room for doubt. "The dishwasher needs to be emptied before 6:00 p.m."

Part of teaching children to obey involves giving them choices—and outlining consequences. "If you do so-and-so, the consequences will be thus-and-such." Then stick to your guns and follow through. Consistency is one of the hardest things, especially for exhausted parents, but one of the most important. If your children couldn't do it yesterday, when they ask again today, tomorrow, and next week, the response better be the same.

"I wanted my children to obey me because they loved me, but an elderly preacher told me it doesn't work that way," recalls Elizabeth Guenther, who raised six children. "Instead, he told me I should speak once and then have my children repeat the command. If they said it incorrectly, I should look them in the eye and repeat it again." That method ensured her children knew exactly what the expectations were. If they chose to disobey, they also learned about consequences.

Don't be afraid to let your children feel guilty for disobedience, either. I've talked with many parents who feel guilt is somehow a bad thing. Not always. There is a place for remorse. We teach our children how to deal with the natural consequences of their actions. If we don't also teach them about the emotional consequences of poor choices—guilt and remorse—we've neglected an important element in their training.

Obviously it is better to start expecting obedience early, but it is never too late to start. Even if your children are older, showing them by your actions that you mean what you say is the key to obedience. Kids need and want limits—despite ranting and raving to the contrary. They want to know where the lines are. It's our job as parents to set those boundaries for them, so that someday they can set boundaries for themselves. I've heard that if your kids are always happy with you, you're not doing it right. Given how much flak we get, my husband and I figure we're on the right track.

The Respect Connection

Over the years, I spent a great deal of time working with the children and teens at our local church. I taught

Sunday school, worked in the AWANA program, and led the youth choir and drama program. As the years passed, the same kids I once towered over dwarfed my five-foot, two-inch height. But they still respected me, and it had nothing to do with my size. When six-foot kids defied me, the only way I could get them to obey was through my position—and the respect they had for it and for me. I couldn't physically force the kids to do anything. But they respected me and my position as a leader.

One of the reasons for this is that the kids knew I meant what I said. I hated to do it, but I had to prove that publicly once or twice. It was a lesson they remembered. Kids know instinctively whom they can push and who will stand firm. They need a combination of unconditional love for who they are as people and clear limits on their behavior.

Sue Wright realized how much her attitude toward her son would affect his respect for her.

"I learned my most important parenting lesson early in my son, Richard's, life. I became a single parent when he was two years old, and I realized he had to obey me because he loved and respected me, not because I would punish him. I knew that when he became sixteen, he could knock me down and stomp on me if he was raised with constant physical punishment, so there had to be a better way of discipline: respect and love for each other.

"I learned this lesson at great cost. Shortly after my divorce, when my son was going through the terrible twos (and threes), we had a disagreement about something. He stomped away to his room, screaming, 'I am going to run away from home.'

"I told him, 'OK, let me help you pack.' We threw a few clothes in a suitcase, and I sent him out the door at nearly dark.

"When I saw that precious little boy going down the sidewalk, carrying his suitcase, I came to my senses. I called him back, hugged and kissed him, and explained to him there wasn't anything so bad that we could not work it out. I told him, 'This is your home and my home. We are both going to live here together, and we can live happily. If we become angry with each other, we will talk about it and work it out.'

"Everything was not entirely rosy throughout the years, but we did, and still do, have a mutual respect and great love for each other. He is forty-one years old now and probably does not remember that incident; however, I DO. Even as I recount this today, I am openly weeping."

Through this situation, Sue set up the framework for, and expectation of, respect in their home. And like the Taylors, she also demonstrated to her son that facing tough situations together—not running away in anger—is the right response to conflict.

If you set clear limits on behavior, and then back those up with a balance of love, control, and consequences, you will instill in your children a lifelong respect for your authority.

The Power of No

"Saying yes as much as possible is one of the most basic principles of parenting," say Connie Grigsby and Kent Julian, authors of *How to Get Your Teen to Talk to You*. They also point out that when you do say yes often, it makes the occasional no easier to hear.[6]

But there's the rub. While yes is important for kids to hear, the opposite is equally necessary. Too many parents don't ever tell their children no. They fear frustrating their children or in some way "squelching their personalities," as comedian Mark Lowry puts it. Yet frustration is a normal part of life and something our children must learn to deal with properly. Once our kids are out on their own, they'll be told no quite a bit. Our job is to teach them how to deal with it. Saying no does that.

Greg Hattaway says that while their son, Doug, was in high school, he and his wife realized that sometimes kids desperately need parents to say no. They may even come right out and say so.

"One night Doug called home and said that he was with some friends and that they wanted to go somewhere other than where he had told us he was going. There was a period of silence, and then Doug said, 'Tell me no.' So, I said no.

"When he got home, he said that the rest of the boys wanted to go somewhere he felt he shouldn't go, and even though all their parents had agreed (apparently after some less-than-truthful conversations), he did not want to do likewise. Sometimes, they really do want you to tell them no."

You know your children and their maturity level as well as their areas of weakness. We have often reminded our children that we are happy to be the "bad guys" in situations where they need help. If they're invited somewhere and we sense a real hesitation on their part, we'll ask, "Do you need us to say no?" Sometimes that is exactly what they need. We've also let them know that if they ever find themselves somewhere they shouldn't be, or in a situation that isn't what they expected, we are only a phone call away. Don't hesitate to ask questions like, "Do you need us to come get you?" or, "What would you say if you were me?"

All children need to hear no on occasion. Knowing we can and will act in their best interests—even if they don't like it—gives them security and trust in us as their parents.

Choose Your Battles

While my children were younger, I frequently heard more-experienced parents say, "Choose your battles." Now that our kids are both teens, the truth of that statement has come home in a big way. Part of a teen's normal development is to pull away from parents to find his or her identity. That often means your child looks, acts, sounds, and dresses differently every week. Friends get replaced faster than empty milk cartons. And making the shift from controlling everything in a young child's life to choosing which things to exercise control over in your teen's life is not always that simple.

If control is a big thing for you, this part will be hard. Take a long, hard look at your beliefs and values, and decide which issues are critical and which are temporary issues or questions of preference. If this situation won't even be remembered next week, let alone next year, it may not be worth fighting over. However, if it's something that could impact your child's life forever, stand firm. Realize that hair color and questions of honesty and integrity are not in the same category. Decide which things matter in the long run, and don't budge on those issues.

Dr. James Dobson calls this the "Loosen and Tighten Principle." In his book *Parenting Isn't for Cowards*, he says that when their children became teenagers, they tried to "loosen [their] grip on everything that had no lasting significance, and tighten down on everything that did."[7]

Be proactive in your parenting. Recently, my husband and I talked about the next few years and how we'll respond if and when certain questions come up. How will you handle tattoos, blue hair, and piercings? How about dating, driving, and after-school jobs?

When you have decisions clearly thought out ahead of time, you won't be caught off guard later. Then you'll respond in a clear, nonemotional way, which is far more effective than an off-the-cuff, explosive "Are you nuts?"

Teaching Self-Control

I remember a cartoon from years ago that showed a little boy sitting in the corner. He looked over his shoulder and said something like, "I may be sitting on the outside, but I'm standing on the inside."

That makes me smile every time I think of it, because it shows the beginnings of self-control. When it comes to this issue, almost every parenting book I consulted had something similar to say. It all boils down to this: self-control is what obedience is all about. It means teaching our children to do the outward action we require, despite their internal disagreement.

Like most things, this is easier said than done, for parents and children. During my teen years, I once asked my mother if I could go somewhere with friends, and she said no. No reason, no explanation, no justification that I could see. Clearly she was just being mean. So I reacted badly. I ranted and raved and cried, and still the answer remained no. (I obviously needed a refresher on the mom-means-what-she-says rule.)

After I'd finally calmed down, Mom came into my room and said something I've never forgotten. "You know, I was planning to say yes, but I said no to see how you would react."

My mouth dropped open. I was furious all over again, but now I was angrier than I'd been before. How could she do this to me? Didn't she know how important this was? "All this was some kind of test?" I screeched.

"It was," she said. "Sometimes the answer will be yes, and sometimes the answer will be no, and you have to be able to deal with both." Because I reacted badly, the answer stayed no.

The next time she said no, I bit my tongue and responded without heat, hoping this was another test. When she assured me it wasn't, that the answer was still no, I had to fight that internal battle all over again. But you can be sure that I was careful to have my emotions in check before I asked.

Someday when a boss gives your children an assignment they don't want to do, or a teacher assigns a project they can't stand the idea of working on, self-control will help them respond correctly. It's the old mind-over-matter. Self-control means acting in the right way, responding correctly, even though our feelings say something different. It requires skill and practice to learn to respond based on facts rather than on feelings. Smart parents teach their children the difference. When we tell our children no, they have a choice to make on how they will respond. Will they react on pure emotion? Or will they be able to calm themselves and think through their response first?

Like many teen girls, my instinctive reaction to most things I didn't like was tears, complete with great, gasping sobs. If Dad said something I didn't like, I'd hunt him down to plead my case. As long as I kept my emotions under control and presented my case clearly and logically, he listened. But as soon as I slid into tearful pleas, he sent me to my room. "When you have yourself under control, come back and we'll talk some more."

In different ways, both parents taught me great lessons in self-control. I learned what worked and what didn't and the right and wrong ways to try to get what I wanted.

Modeling Self-Control

Especially in emotionally charged situations, it is critical that parents stay in control of themselves too. Your children will not learn to speak in a reasonable tone if you screech. There is a German saying that we use a lot at our house: *Der Ton macht die Musik*. It means "the tone makes the music"—it isn't what we say but how we say it. My facial expression and tone of voice have a huge impact on how my words are received.

If things begin to get heated and you think you or your child is in danger of losing control, don't hesitate to declare a time-out for both parties to cool off. Set a time and then meet back together to continue the discussion. This teaches volumes about self-control, conflict resolution, and how to make wise choices.

Do as I Say . . .

Life would be much easier if our kids learned only from what we say—not from what we do. But our children absorb far more from our actions than our words. So how are we doing in the area of teaching our children to respect authority?

Ask yourself these questions:

- Do my children respect my authority and obey me—even when they don't like it?
- Are the rules and expectations in our household clearly defined?
- Are the consequences for breaking house rules also clear?
- If my children defy what I've said, do I stand firm and follow through? Or do I back down and give in?
- Have I let my children know that I mean what I say?
- How have I done that? (Give an example.)
- Have I taught them BY EXAMPLE to obey those in authority? (List practical examples.)
- How do they hear me talk about my boss?
- Do my children know I do my best at work—even if I think the request is unreasonable?
- How do they hear me talk about political figures?
- Do I pray for our leaders at least as much as I criticize them?
- How seriously do I take the traffic laws?
- Do I elbow my way to the front of the line?
- Do I live as though the rules don't apply to me?
- How do I view God's authority over my life? In what way do I communicate that to my children?

- Do they see me ask God for wisdom and guidance?
- Have they ever seen me *on my knees*?

If you have late elementary/middle school children:

- When did I last tell my children no?
- What issue did my children last test the limits on? Did I stand firm?
- Have I reminded my children lately that they are not in charge?
- Have I taught my children to deal with the phrase, "Because I said so"?
- Do I have a call-anytime support agreement with my spouse or a friend to help me stand firm in the face of child pressure?
- Have I reminded my children lately that just as they answer to me, I answer to God for how I parent?

If you have older teens:

- Have my spouse and I thought through which things we feel are moral issues and which are preferences? Make a list, decide which category things fit into, and then compare notes.
- Have we as parents decided how we'll handle questions about tattoos, piercings, blue hair, and similar things?
- List the "Can I do this?" questions you know are coming and how you'll respond to them.
- Have I ever asked my teens if I needed to help them by saying no in a particular situation?

- Have I reminded my teens of the respect-for-authority standard in our family when they've tried to cross the line?
- Do my teens know the right—and wrong—way to approach me when trying to get their way?

2

Show Me the Money

Recently I asked a group of parents whose children are grown and gone to answer two questions:

1) What are the three most important things you taught your children?
2) What's the one thing you didn't teach them that you wish you had?

The responses I received were wonderful. Some of the things these parents had taught their children included honesty, discipline, and manners; how to love and how to work; to love the Lord and to laugh often; to forgive and to care for others; to do their best; and to respect their parents and to respect all people, regardless of race or background. One dad's top-three list of things he'd taught his children included one item conspicuously absent from most of the other respondents' lists: how to handle personal finances and pay all bills on time.

I was surprised to find that money management was the number-one thing the parents I surveyed wish they'd taught their children. My first guess would have been sex, but statistics show that finances and sex are the two least-talked-about things in families. That tells us money management is a critical area we need to address in our homes.

Kids live for today; that's part of their mind-set at this point in their lives. Their inability to look further down the road of life than Friday night is why so many parents have prematurely gray hair. Before we know it, the same kid who blows all his birthday money in an afternoon at the music store is going to have to pay rent and buy his own groceries. How can we adequately prepare our children to handle their finances?

As in most parenting issues, the buck, literally, stops here. Children will carry into adulthood both the values and habits they've seen modeled in the home. But when it comes to money management, they also need some deliberate, hands-on teaching and experience. Again, if we don't teach them, how will they know?

The Allowance Question

Mary Hunt, in her book *Debt-Proof Living*, says the debt-proof–living formula is this: 10-10-80. Simply put, of every dollar that comes our way, we give away 10 percent, save 10 percent, and live on 80 percent. And we do it in exactly that order.[1] But before we can give or save, we have to have some money. Children's first regular income source is usually an allowance. Since there has been much debate on this topic, I'll simply give you our family's view on it and let you decide.

At our house, receiving an allowance and doing chores are not tied together. Our children don't get paid for doing regular chores, and they don't get to decide if they want to do them or not. If we said they'd get paid for whatever chores they did, nine times out of ten they'd gladly forgo the money so they wouldn't have to work. We believe chores and household responsibilities are part of being a good family citizen. They are not optional.

We sometimes pay them for doing things that are beyond the norm, like cleaning out the garage or painting, but those situations are the exception, not the rule. When I was growing up, Mom regularly gave me the opportunity to earn money by pulling weeds. However, this "opportunity" was not optional; it was required. Given the choice, I'd have forgone the money in a heartbeat, because I hated weeding (sorry, Mom). Whether you want to make additional chores optional or not is up to you.

As your children get older, increase their allowance, and require that they use it to pay for certain things. That is the first step toward teaching money management. Some parents argue that the best plan is simply to give kids money whenever they need it. That's tempting, especially because then they can't blow it all on something frivolous. But if children aren't given opportunities to make decisions—even bad ones—now, they may make some down the road that will haunt them forever.

To help your children learn to look ahead, set a regular payday—and stick to it. That means parents have to plan ahead too, which has been a challenge at our house. You may have to be firm when pleas for loans and advances become deafening. To give our children an even bigger taste of life in the real world, we've been spreading out the time between payments as they get older.

Giving Comes First

As soon as your children begin receiving any sort of income, you should begin teaching them the importance of tithing. If this has not been a regular part of your life, you may instantly protest that you can't possibly give any money away, but as Mary Hunt says, "The very act of giving is an expression of gratitude. It is a tangible way I can say thank-you for everything I have and for every way I have been blessed."[2]

From the time our children were very young, we've taught them that everything we have belongs to God. He allows us to use it, and he wants us to be good stewards of it. We believe part of that means giving a portion of it—at least 10 percent—back to him for use in his work around the world.

Even if you've never done this personally before, start now. Maybe start small, at, say, 2 or 3 percent, and work up from there. Ask God to give you the courage to be faithful in this area. It is very much a question of trust, a belief that if we honor God in this way, he'll enable us to live on what's left. And be sure to include your children in the process. Make sure they know you give, and begin giving them opportunities to do the same.

It is easy to fish around in your pocket for some loose change and press it into your toddler's hand before Sunday school, but it will be much more meaningful—and a much greater teaching opportunity—if that nickel or dime comes from her money instead of yours. Be clear in your explanations and expectations. Georgia Taylor remembered a time she and her husband had to set the record straight with one of their boys.

"When Timothy was just a little thing, we started teaching him about tithing and about how we give God 10 percent of everything we have. Every Sunday morning, we'd give him a bit of money to put in the offering in Sunday school. After a while, we realized that he'd always come home with change a'jingling in his pocket. When we asked if he'd given that money in church like he was supposed to, he said, 'Yes, I did.'

"Well, we just couldn't figure out where that extra money came from. Finally we asked him if he gave ALL the money we gave him every Sunday morning. He said, 'No. I gave 10 percent, just like you said.'

"We had to tell him that 10 percent is the bare minimum, the least we can give, and that God expects us to give beyond that."

Be creative. Look around your church and community for opportunities for giving: missionaries, the local homeless shelter or soup kitchen, special-needs fundraisers, and more.

Remember the story of the widow's mite? She gave a few little coins, but it was all she had; Jesus valued that much more highly than the flashy contributions made by those who wanted everyone to see how generous they were. It was the widow's heart attitude that made the difference.

If you start when your children are very young and keep providing them with opportunities to earn some money and then give it themselves, you'll start building a lifelong open-hand attitude toward financial stewardship. Teach your children the joy of giving. Lead by example.

In conjunction with financial giving, remember that giving and tithing is about more than money. Part of giving freely can mean time or possessions too. It's about an open-handed approach to everything in our lives. Our kids have given favorite toys to children in need and duplicate winter clothing to those who had none.

It takes practice to learn to hold our possessions loosely. In our gimme-gimme society, cultivating a mind-set that doesn't hoard is difficult. But if we view ourselves as the manager of what we've been given, rather than the sole owner, it is easier to loosen our grip. This doesn't mean being unwise, but it does mean losing the Ebenezer Scrooge miser mentality. Find a healthy balance. God gives us money to spend. How we spend it says volumes about our priorities.

I want to share with you something that has become our family tradition, not to pat ourselves on the back but to help spark some creative ideas in your family and to tell you what a difference it has made in ours.

Several years ago, our extended family realized that even though we'd cut down on Christmas buying by drawing names for the adults and only buying multiple gifts for the children, Christmas was still putting a huge strain on everyone's budget, since we have a fairly good-sized family. Plus, we reasoned, how much more stuff do any of us *really* need?

So we tried something radical. We still drew names for the adults, but we decided that the gift could cost no more than ten dollars, which meant using a bit of creativity. Then we researched several relief agencies and found one whose work we admired. On Christmas Eve, after the gifts were distributed, we passed a basket around, and everyone contributed whatever they wanted to the fund.

At first, we each gave what we'd otherwise have spent on gifts, but now that we know it's coming, we put a bit aside throughout the year as well.

The agency provides a catalog of ministries and the various needs they have, so we go around the room, and each family member, from the youngest to the oldest, gets to pick something he or she would like to see us spend part of our fund toward. Once the wish list is compiled, we allocate how the money will be spent and send the money in. It has been amazing to watch family members choose those needs closest to their hearts. And as a family, we've had the privilege of feeling a part of God's work in many corners of the world.

The Savings Solution

If you haven't already done so, open savings accounts with your children. Many banks offer them for free. Right now, our children have minor accounts, which means I'm still the custodian, so they can't empty the account without my say-so. But for each birthday, they know a portion of the money they receive must go into the account. They enjoy seeing how quickly a little bit can add up.

To avoid having the savings account feel like a black hole into which your children pour money they'll never see again, set up short- and long-term savings goals. Decide when the money goes in and when some can come out. A short-term goal might be a new bike or stereo or video game. A long-term goal might be a car or college tuition or the security deposit and first three months' rent for an apartment. The older the child, the more input he or she should have.

Besides a regular savings account, there are many investment opportunities and ways to make money grow. I don't have space here to go into this topic at length, but rest assured it isn't as scary as it sounds. Many excellent resources are available on the subject, a few of which are listed at the end of this book. If your family hasn't done much investing, consider making it a family project, and begin learning the ropes together.

A Spending Plan

Once you've talked about giving and saving, take a few minutes to decide what things you will give your child both the money and the responsibility to buy. The older the child is, the greater the allowance and the longer the list. Your list might include gifts for family and friends, school lunches, haircuts, school supplies and fees (including field trips and sports team expenses), toiletries (above the family supply), CDs, books, computer and video games (both rental and purchase), and movies. Avoid the temptation to advance money or make exceptions, for those will quickly turn into expectations.

Also, if you haven't already, start talking with your children about how much "real-life" things cost. Once our children hit middle school, cars became a high-interest item. We began scanning the classifieds for new and used cars, which also gave us an opportunity to talk about how much we pay for gas every month. They were also surprised to learn that we pay a certain amount every month for car insurance, whether we drive the car or not.

Teach your teen to review the check and calculate the tip when you go to a restaurant. It's a great way to combine math skills with a little lesson on generosity and the right way to treat those in service professions.

When your kids' eyes begin to light up at all manner of electronic devices, introduce your kids to magazines like *Consumer Reports*, which review almost anything you can think of, to help them make wise choices. Sometimes the lowest-priced item is not the best deal in the long run, and conversely, the highest-priced item is not always the best quality.

The Clothes Caper

The older children get, the more peer pressure figures into the buying decision—at least as far as clothing is concerned. For older teens, one practical way to help break through this barrier is to decide on a clothing budget and then let your teens buy their own clothes. If you're worried they'll blow the whole wad on name-brand jeans, you may decide you'll buy them a warm jacket or Sunday dress, for instance. But be clear on what items they will be expected to pay for out of that budget.

To further teach teens about budgeting, figure out how much you usually spend on their clothing in a year, divide the amount up, and give it to them several times throughout the year. When the money's gone, that's it, no matter who's having a party or what occasion they forgot to figure in. Also, you might want to let them know that any money not spent on clothing gets returned to you. They don't get to keep it. Otherwise, your teens may not buy anything new in order to buy a new electronic gizmo or gadget.

Scary though this is for parents, expect that your teens will make some mistakes. Let them. Small mistakes now will avoid bigger ones later.

By the way, I tell my children that they may choose their own clothing, but we still have veto power. By now they know our standards for modesty and appropriateness and can pretty well guess what things we'd make them return. We give refresher courses when necessary. (More on clothing standards in chapter 8.)

Once teens begin price comparisons and trying to make their clothing budget stretch as far as possible, you'll be amazed at how differently they view the whole clothing issue. One day our son was sitting in the high school cafeteria when an upperclassman strolled over and said, "Hey, dude. Cool jeans. Where did you get them?"

Without blinking Ben replied, "Wal-Mart." The kid made a dismissive noise and walked away. Ben and his friends thought the whole thing was pretty funny. His jeans were considered cool until the kid knew where they came from. "But I only paid half what a brand-name pair costs," he said.

My daughter caught the thrift-store bug when she realized how much further her clothing dollars would reach. Garage sales are another great source for clothes. The idea of shopping at these places will become more appealing to your teens when the money comes out of their pockets.

Filling the Hollow Leg

Unless your children go with you to the grocery store and learn to shop, they will never grasp how much food costs. Even though the trip will take longer, take your kids with you to the grocery store, at least occasionally.

When ours were in elementary school, I had them help me with small tasks. I'd send them down the cereal aisle and tell them each to pick out a box. But I wanted to know how much it cost, how big the box was, and why they chose that one over another one.

Even though they were young, they were amazed at how much we spent on food. It didn't take them long to figure out that generic cereal tasted pretty much the same as brand-name, only the store brand cost about half the price of the other. That meant for the same price, they'd get twice as much cereal. This became an easy way to begin teaching them to comparison shop and how to get the most bang for the buck.

Checking Accounts and ATM Cards

When your older teens begin a regular job or have regular income, go with them to open a checking account. It is important to teach them not only how to write checks, but how to reconcile the account. Otherwise they might sound like the sign I saw: "How can I be out of money if I still have checks left?" That little quip may make us smile, but bounced checks are no laughing matter. A good credit rating is hard to establish but easy to ruin.

You will also have to decide if and when your children are ready to handle an ATM card and what the withdrawal limits will be. The deciding factor for getting an ATM card should be maturity level, because those cards can be dangerous things. Yes, they're convenient, but because they delude us into thinking we have an unlimited supply of cash, they can also lead the unwary financially astray.

At a bare minimum, your children must know to keep the card in a safe place and guard it as though it were cash. They should never give their PIN to friends, not even their very best friends in the whole world. Suzie or Billy may well be their very worst enemy by week's end. Set a daily withdrawal limit so that if the card does somehow fall into the wrong hands, the financial damage would be relatively minimal. And though your teens will probably roll their eyes, warn them often to check who's around when they approach an ATM machine, especially at night.

Our Instant-Gratification Society

In our world, we want everything today—whether we can afford it or not. Too many families live paycheck to paycheck, spending not only what they earn, but more than what they earn by using credit cards. If you have a mound of unsecured debt, by all means, do whatever is necessary to get out from under it. (Mary Hunt's *Debt-Proof Living* is a good place to start.) Then teach your children the wise and cautious use of credit, so they won't get caught in the same trap.

One mother I spoke with said they'd spent a good bit of time teaching their daughter about the dangers of credit cards and spending money she didn't have. When the daughter went to college, she was shocked to see credit card company booths crowded around the campus registration area, with students lined up to get the cards. The girl told her mother she wanted to run up to these kids and shout, "Didn't your parents warn you about this stuff?" Today credit card companies are on almost every college campus, trying to lure uninformed students with the promise of low minimum payments. Make sure your kid isn't lured in.

For some things, like renting a car, a credit card will be necessary, so teach your children how to use credit wisely. The first step for an older teen would be a store credit card. These generally have low credit lines and will teach your children to balance the joy of making the purchase with the reality of paying the bill.

Stress over and over and over that they should never buy something unless they have the money to pay for it. The Bible makes it clear that we should owe no one anything and that the borrower is servant to the lender (Rom. 13:8, Prov. 22:7). Teach your children that *hoping* they'll have the money by the time the bill arrives is not good enough. And if they get into trouble, don't bail them out by paying the debt for them. Instead, help them find ways to pay it off themselves. It's a lesson they will never forget.

Honesty Matters

It seems all the parents I know admit to stealing something when they were little and remember having to deal with it when their own children tried to get by with it. Our two were still toddlers when it happened to us. We were in one of those grocery stores with the bulk bins where you can scoop candy and nuts into your own little bag. Ben begged for gummy worms. I said no. I reached for something on a shelf, turned back, and there he was, little cheeks puffed out and the tail of one worm still dangling from the corner of his mouth. When I asked if he'd taken the worms, he shook his head no, making that little worm tail flop back and forth. When I said I knew he had taken them, he mumbled, "But Michele did too."

Michele couldn't even reach the shelf, so I knew she was not the instigator of this little caper. I took a crying Ben to the cashier and made him tell the lady that he'd taken something that didn't belong to him. It was a lesson he never forgot. Unless someone offers it to him, he won't take so much as a walnut from a store.

Single mom Patty Stephens tells of a similar situation when her son was in elementary school.

"While we were in the store one day, Jimmy asked me to buy him some green grenade balloons, which were a really hot item back then. When I said no, he asked if he could go look at the things in the next aisle.

"Later, on the ride home, I looked over and thought, *What is that?* Sure enough, several green grenade balloons were sticking out of his pants pocket. I read him the riot act, up one side and down the other, about how stealing was wrong and that we don't ever take things that don't belong to us. Jimmy said, 'But I only took two, not the whole box.'

"I pulled over, whipped the car around, and marched that boy back into the store, right up to the store manager. I made Jimmy tell the man what he'd done. The manager was very gracious about the whole thing, but Jimmy was mortified and hated having to confess that he'd taken those balloons. Afterward I said to him, 'Personal responsibility starts here. We don't steal.'"

Of course, you have to be careful that you practice what you preach. My kids and I were in a department store one day, and as I flipped through the blouses, I would grab "possibles" and hook the hanger on my arm as I went through the rack. The kids were playing nearby, and I noticed them scooping up those white, numbered clips stores put over hangers so you can tell the item's size. I told them those belonged to the store and made them put the clips back.

We had left the store and were walking through the mall when I noticed that both children had bulging pants pockets. When I questioned them, both reluctantly pulled out handfuls of those little tags. There I stood, in the middle of the mall, shaking my finger and scolding them for stealing, when I suddenly looked down . . . and saw those four blouses still hanging on my arm. Oh no! Quick as we could, we returned both the blouses AND the little number tags to the store. And I had an opportunity to explain to the children that taking what doesn't belong to you is wrong—even if you didn't do it on purpose.

But You've Always Done It

Since kids generally live up to the expectations we set for them, think through the patterns you may unknowingly be creating in your family. If you are always the family ATM, doling out money to your children every time they need it, they will be in for a rude awakening when they leave home. It is far better to slowly, carefully, shift the responsibility to their shoulders.

Also, be careful of being harsh when your children make a money mistake. Haven't we all made them? Instead, use this as an opportunity to help your children plan ways to do better next time.

When I got out of college, I was absolutely astonished to meet so many people in their midtwenties who owed twenty-two thousand to twenty-five thousand dollars to credit card companies. We're not talking student loans or car payments here—just credit card debt. When

I asked what they had bought, most shrugged their shoulders. "Just stuff." With some advance planning, we can make sure our children are never in that position. Let's help them start their future on solid financial footing.

As you prepare your children financially, here are some questions you need to ask yourself:

- Do we follow the 10-10-80 formula in our household?
- Do my children see me give charitably?
- Am I requiring that they give a specified percentage of their income to a cause or organization I approve of?
- Is their money kept in a specific place for safekeeping?
- Have I established a defined allowance amount and "payday"?
- Do I help my children analyze the value of certain items? ("How long will it last?" "Is it worth four weeks of babysitting?")
- Do I allow my children to suffer the pain of poor money choices?
- Have I discussed the advantages and pitfalls of buying on credit?
- Have I taught my children how to calculate interest and shown them the benefits of long-term savings?
- Do they understand the basics of investing?
- Do they know how to follow a budget?

If you have late elementary/middle school children:

- Have I given my children clear instructions regarding which items they are responsible to pay for?
- Do I regularly hand out "just a little more"?
- Do I regularly advance allowance money? (If so, you may have to rethink the amount or what it covers.)
- Do I give my children opportunities to see the cost of things in the family budget?
- Does part of all the money my child receives get saved? Where?
- Does my child have a savings account?
- Have I outlined what that money can be used for?
- Does my child tithe a portion of all his income?

If you have older teens:

- Does my child check the bill and calculate the tip at a restaurant?
- Does she know the cost of car insurance? When she starts driving, have I made clear who will pay for it?
- Have I outlined budget items and what I'll pay for and what is the child's responsibility?
- Does my teen buy his own clothes within a certain budget?
- If my child has a job, does she also have a checking account?
- Have I taught him how to balance it?

3

Personal Responsibility and Self-Discipline

Our local high school updated the dress code again this school year, as it does most years. The new list of thou-shalt-nots was longer and more specific, with the most notable change a prohibition against unnatural-colored hair. This caused a flurry of phone calls and complaints among the students, which wasn't unusual, since that happens every year too. What changed was the attitude of the students, parents, and administration.

I was with several parents and teens, exchanging various dress-code-violation stories, when one student said, "But it's really not that big a deal. If you get written up for dress code and the school calls your parents, if your parents complain and make a big deal about it, the school won't say anything about it anymore."

"So the school won't enforce the policy if your parents make a fuss?" I asked. Apparently that's how it works.

Back in 1881, T. H. Huxley said, "Logical consequences are the scarecrows of fools and the beacons of wise men."[1] Sadly, by protecting their children from logical consequences, these parents are raising irresponsible, no-fault children. They are perpetuating the belief that everything is somebody else's fault, from unfair dress codes and too-hot coffee at McDonald's to fast food making people fat. It seems that old problem from Eden—passing the buck—is alive and well. So how do we raise responsible kids in a no-fault world? By teaching them personal accountability and self-discipline.

Start Small

One of the basics of personal responsibility is getting out of bed every morning. By the time your children reach fourth grade, they should have an alarm clock and be in charge of getting out of bed—on their own. This quickly ends those endless rounds of parental nagging and cajoling and starts shifting more responsibility onto their shoulders. When you treat your children as though they are capable individuals, they will rise to the challenge and feel more confident too.

School lunches are another basic responsibility. There is no reason fourth graders can't pack their own lunches. You may need to provide guidelines of what that lunch should include, but the planning and packing of the food should be your children's responsibility. We set up requirements that include fruit and/or veggies.

Both of these areas also provide opportunities to teach children about actions and logical consequences. At our house, our children each get one free homework/lunch delivery by Mom each semester, plus one ride to school. Bad weather, bulky projects, and so forth don't count in that number. These freebies are because everyone occasionally forgets something or gets behind schedule, but there is only one, so everyone understands these are the exception and not the rule.

After their allotted freebies, my kids don't even bother calling home to ask for an exception. They know they won't get it. If they forget to make lunch, well, then they pay out of their allowance or go hungry. By the way, lest this sound too harsh, it only happened once with each of our children. After that, they understood that we meant what we said about personal responsibility. We also saw their confidence increase as they learned to handle these areas on their own.

Whose Turn Is It?

We'll talk more about the specifics of chores in chapter 4, but for now, I want to mention their importance in teaching children responsibility. Since children don't get excited about work, especially work that brings no tangible reward that they can see, expect complaints. Simply reiterating the wonders of working together as a family aren't likely to end the griping. You'll have to stand firm. Houses and apartments do not clean themselves; that's the responsibility of those who live in them. Hence, all residents will contribute to keeping things clean and organized. And yes, you may have to say that sixteen times every day until everyone realizes you mean it.

When you set responsibilities, keep the age of the children in mind, and outline consequences for not doing the work. That makes it clear that chores aren't optional. They're a requirement for every family member. When your children whine, "But why do we have to?" gently remind them that you're the parent and God says children need to honor their father and mother. After everyone finishes ranting and raving over the unfairness of that, follow up with the old standby: because I said so.

Also make it clear to your children how things are prioritized in your family. We've told our children that school is their job and primary responsibility right now. On nights when they've been swamped with homework, we have sometimes helped them out with chores a bit to ease the stress. But be careful, or they'll pick up on that faster than you can blink and forever after have some reason why they can't do their household jobs. It's a careful balance: responsibility and grace.

The Replacement Rule

You've seen the signs in stores: you break it; you bought it. Make that part of your family philosophy as well. If your child breaks or loses someone else's stuff, he must replace it—with his money. This applies to possessions belonging to friends *and* relatives. Princess will think twice about breaking a sibling's prized toy in a fit of rage if she knows she'll have to replace it on her own nickel.

The same thing goes for their own stuff: if your children break or lose their possessions, make sure they understand that they will have to buy replacements or do without. We've made this especially clear about jackets, because they get left in the most unlikely places. If your children know the consequences for losing things ahead of time, they'll be much more careful about seeing that items get home again.

For several summers, our son went north to visit family with a new pair of flip-flops and came home without them. One year, he had to buy a new pair when he got home—out of his money. He hasn't lost a pair since.

Of course, there are legitimate accidents or times when the loss or destruction of something was truly beyond our children's control. Evaluate the situation carefully. There is a fine line, but the goal is always to teach our children to take responsibility—for their actions and their possessions.

All of us tend to value most the things that cost us something. If we buy our children whatever they want and make everything too easy for them, they will never learn to place value on things. A new CD player they worked two weekends to pay for will be more valuable to them than one you purchased for them on impulse.

Eeny Meeny Miney Moe

Children have to learn to make good choices. Part of that means occasionally learning from bad choices. As your children mature, they need to gradually take on more and more of their day-to-day decision making. First they'll learn to pick out their own clothing, and later they'll learn how to budget their time, money, and activities. By learning to decide the little things with confidence, they will eventually be ready to make big decisions with equal ease.

A simple choice might be telling a young child she is allowed to have one ice pop every day. She can decide when she wants to eat it, but she only gets one. The first day, that ice pop may be gone by 8:30 a.m., and Princess will be begging for another when the rest of the family eats theirs after dinner. Stand firm and remind her that she made her choice and now the rest of you are making yours. Next time, she'll think it through a bit more carefully before she decides.

Or you could tell Junior that he can watch one hour of TV on any given day (within parental guidelines), but he can only choose one. After that, he must leave the room and do something else. If you further say that homework must be completed before the TV goes on, he'll learn even more about choices, responsibility, and planning. And if he tries to sneak around the rules and watch TV before he does his homework, then he'll lose his TV privileges for a while.

Choices have consequences, good and bad, and since they're part of everyday life, we must teach our children how to choose well. Start with small decisions and slowly, gradually work up to bigger ones.

The Ticking Clock

Time management is another component of personal responsibility. It obviously ties in with chores and getting out of bed in the morning, but it also becomes critical with regard to homework, specifically school projects—you know, those huge, creativity-required ones science teachers are especially fond of, or the megareports favored by English teachers. Most teachers assign these projects well in advance of the due date. The challenge for children is thinking and planning far enough in advance to avoid eleventh-hour panic the night before the due date. The idea of doing a bit each day is hard for them to grasp.

Usually this concept doesn't really sink in until they've tried—and failed—to come up with a wonderful project following a mad scramble the night before.

So how does a parent handle this? The key is to regularly mention the upcoming project—on a daily basis for an elementary-age child, less often for a middle or high school student. You might also help your child break the project into smaller pieces and set up completion dates for each part on the calendar and then regularly check in on his progress. Sometimes it's the sheer size of the project that paralyzes kids. They simply don't know where or how to start. But here's the really hard part: if your child doesn't do it at all, or gets frustrated and quits in tears in the middle of the night before it's due, don't finish it for him. You may help, you may offer encouragement, but if you're still wielding a glue gun or typing a paper at 2:00 a.m. while your child sleeps, she's not learning anything.

I only did this once. I was tired and frustrated and finally said, "That's it. This is not my job, and by doing it, I'm teaching my child to avoid responsibility."

By middle school, both our children were typing their own papers. In this day and age, keyboarding is a necessary life skill. It's kind of like the old saying: give a man a fish, and you feed him for a day; teach a man to fish, and you feed him for a lifetime.

When it comes to school projects and deadlines, I've adopted a motto from the business world: poor planning on your part does not constitute an emergency on my part. I tell our children that I'm happy to take them to the library or to the store for supplies. However, if they think I'm going to do that at 11:00 p.m. the night before the project is due, they're going to be flat out of luck. It's important that they show some respect for my time and schedule too, so I'm trying to teach them that planning and communication go hand in hand.

If you start young and let your children learn from their time-management mistakes, you teach them to look ahead. It's better for them to get a bad grade on a project now—and then learn to plan better next time—than to later lose a job because they expected to be bailed out at the last minute and mom and dad weren't there to do it.

The Family Calendar

Of course, all this talk of planning ahead frustrates my spur-of-the-moment children. "Mom," they moan, "why do we have to plan a trip to the mall two weeks ahead of time?"

We have a big magnetic calendar on the fridge, and when the children ask this question, I tell them to check the calendar and then tell me when we can go to the mall. When there isn't an open day for two weeks, it pretty much answers that question.

But when we have lots of scheduled-to-the-max weeks, it is time to reevaluate how we spend our time. You may need to do the same. If your kids never see you because you're always at work, church, the ballpark, or (fill in the blank), you're too busy. Your children will see what you think is most important by how you spend your time. That includes deciding where they rate on your priority scale.

Family therapist Jean Lush also struggled with over-scheduling and the conflict between parenting and career. She says she finally had to "forgive myself for my faulty mothering pattern. Today I encourage myself and other parents to evaluate their time commitments outside the home. What involvements are absolutely necessary? Can some commitments wait until another time in life?" Her last question is the one that really got me. "Do my commitments match my priorities?"[2] Ouch.

When our schedules get overloaded, Mom gets frazzled, which probably means Mom barks at everyone. It is not a pretty sight. This is the time to step back and take a long, hard look at what we're doing.

One day when Ben was about four, I had a job interview scheduled. I hadn't worked in several years, so I was a tad stressed by the prospect of going back to work. Now, one of the unchangeable rules of young children is that the more you hurry them along, the slower they go. I had finally, finally gotten both children dressed and fed and was herding them into the car—with frantic glances at my watch every ten seconds.

Ben interrupted my mad dash when he stopped short, planted both fists on his little hips, and asked, "Mommy, is it more important to be on time or to be nice to me?"

Ooh, that pierced my heart. But I was still late—and getting later with every passing second. I would love to say I ignored my watch and ditched the interview, but I didn't. I took a deep breath and said, "Ben honey, Mommy loves you very much, and it is important for me to be nice to you. But when Mommy's late, like now, it is also important for you to help me by *doing what I ask you to do*!"

I learned several valuable lessons that day. I realized that I set the tone for my family. If I get frazzled, they get frazzled, and that's not how I want our family to live. It was also a painful reminder that being late is no excuse for snapping at those I love. Good time management on my part is critical, for how can I teach what I don't live?

Can't Do It All

Time is a limited commodity, so choices are inevitable. Nobody can—or should—do everything. We must teach our children how to say no graciously. Watch your children's faces the first time you tell someone no in order to spend time with them. That simple little word can make a huge difference in their perception of how much they're worth to you.

Saying no is often a struggle for Christians. The needs are so huge, so overwhelming, and so heartbreaking. How can we say no? If we're honest, sometimes pride also plays a part. We get sucked into believing the recruiter who says that we're the only person who can truly do the job well and that if we don't do it, nobody will. Haven't you been there? I have—pride versus guilt and the feeling that we have no choice but to meet every need we possibly can. I've posted this quote by my desk as a reminder when well-meaning recruiters corner me: "Every need is not a calling. If you're wondering whether you have time to squeeze in one more thing, you don't."[3]

To help teach our children this concept, we've limited them to one sport or activity (besides church) per season. My husband and I also evaluate our church commitments annually and decide what we can—and cannot—do the following year. That helps us avoid guilt-induced, knee-jerk yes answers that would play havoc with our family schedule.

Remember that every yes means a no for something else, because there are only so many hours in a day. I worry when parents tell me they never eat a meal to-gether because they're always on the road or at one sports event or other. If you multiply three children by two—or more—sports each, you'll go crazy. Eventually, it becomes a question of the individual's wants versus the good of the whole family. It's okay to set boundaries around family time and the family unit. Your kids need a sense of home, but they won't get it if they're forever in the car.

Remind your children to choose their activity care-fully, because quitting in the middle is not an option. It's a question of integrity.

Whether it's scouting, sports, or something in-between, at some point, your child will probably decide he wants to quit because it's (a) no longer any fun, (b) boring, or (c) a dumb waste of time. Usually, that's exhaustion talking. Some of the sports schedules, especially, can be grueling. You may need to give your kid a break from practice one night, but be careful to make that the rare exception, not the rule.

Both of our kids have played on teams, and both have had the midseason blahs when they're simply worn out. They've also had times when the sport they signed up for turned out not to be their favorite thing. But we stressed that sticking it out was not only a question of loyalty to the team, but of keeping their word. They had to finish the season, but they didn't have to sign up again.

Other families don't take this stance. One young man joined a soccer team and faithfully came to practices and games for the first half of the season. All of a sudden, he quit showing up. He simply vanished without a word. Eventually, the coach (me, at the time) learned that he quit in order to play football. Neither the child nor his parents ever took the time to let me know.

Also, realize that limiting your children's outside activities won't harm them. It will actually help them develop priorities and teach them that family and relationships matter.

Your family's schedule needs "holes" in it to allow for spontaneous fun. Every once in a while, grab everyone and go to a park and play together. Toss a football; hang out. More than one parenting expert has said that true "quality time" with children happens only as a result of huge amounts of quantity time. Surface conversation gives way to deeper connection through the magic of long, uninterrupted hours together.

Someday, your children will have families of their own. How high spending time with their children rates on their priority list will be directly related to how much time you spend with them now.

As you think about making sure your children have learned self-discipline and personal responsibility, ask yourself:

- Do my children have responsibilities around the house?
- Have I set deadlines for completion of weekly/daily responsibilities?
- What happens when deadlines aren't met?
- Do people know they can count on me to do what I've said I would do?
- Do my children see me honoring the commitments I've made to others?
- If I'm on a team, am I faithful in attending practice?
- Do I finish the season?
- Do we have a family calendar?

- Who pays to replace something my child broke or lost?
- Does my life teach my children to be overcommitted?
- Am I always running late and grumpy?
- What activities can I cut from my schedule during this season of my life?

If you have late elementary/middle school children:

- Are my children responsible for getting out of bed in the morning—without my assistance?
- Do my children pack their own school lunches?
- Do my children keep their rooms up according to the standards I've set?
- What are the consequences if my children ignore their household responsibilities?
- How well do I enforce the consequences?
- Do my children get out the door to school on time? Do I make them suffer the natural consequences if they don't?
- Do I regularly bail my children out of homework crises?
- Have I set limits on the number of outside activities my children may participate in?
- When was the last time I gave one of my children my undivided attention?

If you have older teens:

- Have I clearly outlined what kind of homework help I will and will not provide and when?
- Am I typing while my teens sleep?

- Can my teens make good decisions?
- Have I given them the tools to do so?
- Have I helped them pick up the pieces after bad decisions?
- How will I respond when my teen wants to quit the team midseason?
- Do I model good time management?
- Is every family member responsible for posting his or her commitments on the family calendar?
- How much time have I spent hanging out with my teens this week?

4

Chores and Life Skills

I've always thought it would be wonderful to have an organizational wizard like Alice from *The Brady Bunch* living at my house. I'd love to have someone besides me whose job it is to make sure my world is neat and tidy—with zero effort on my part. Then I wake up and realize, "It ain't gonna happen"—not anytime in the coming millennium that I can see. Because of that, I've informed my family—and anyone who comes to visit—that we have a self-cleaning house. Everyone cleans up after his or her own self.

I posted a sign on our fridge that my mother-in-law purchased in Amish country. It reads: "If I cook it, you eat it. If I buy it, you wear it. If I wash it, you put it away. If I clean it, you keep it clean. If I say bedtime, you say goodnight. If I say no, you don't ask why. 'CAUSE I'M THE MOM."

Right after the sign went up, a friend of Ben's came over and started reading it. The more he read, the bigger his eyes got, and finally he said, "Boy, I'm glad my mom doesn't have a sign like that."

I smiled and said, "Oh, that can be arranged."

I called his mother, a close friend of mine, and read her the sign, and she said, "Oooh, I like that. I'll have to make one too."

I love that sign because it quickly covers a lot of parenting ground. Authority. Expectations. Respect. Our children won't appreciate it now, but learning to respect our authority and doing what we tell them—especially when it comes to working around the house—also develops a critical by-product: life skills. Mastering a full complement of these basics is necessary for life beyond the nest. No one but you will teach your children basics like Laundry 101.

Do I Have To?

I regularly talk with parents who wonder if doing chores is really that big a deal. Do we really need to require it of our children? It seems like a lot of work for the parents. The kids whine and complain, and many parents are just too tired to listen to the gripes. Then there is the fact that the kids don't do a good job, so the parents end up redoing the chores anyway. Why bother? they ask.

In this case, the easier path is not the best path, at least not in the long run. As a therapist, Jean Lush worked with men who were regularly unemployed and couldn't seem to hold down a job for any length of time. She ultimately discovered the common denominator: "These men were never required to work around the house when they were growing up. They were never taught to responsibly and efficiently complete a chore."[1]

Think about that. What better way to prepare our children for a future job than to teach them how to work at home? Also, by contributing to the household and the running of it, children lose their annoying-but-normal sense of entitlement and gain a sense of belonging and accomplishment.

Understand that when you assign chores, especially if you haven't done so in the past, your ears will ring with indignant protests. "But why should I have to do it? That's your job."

When our children were younger, we said, "You will help because you live here and we are all responsible for taking care of our home. I've done it in the past, and now it's time for you to learn to do it. Someday I won't be here to do it for you."

The indignation level seems to rise with age, but we still expect obedience. We now respond, "I was not asking your opinion or making a suggestion; I was telling you how it is. I understand you don't like it, but you will do it anyway. Your attitude about it is your choice."

Chores also teach children early on that work is the way to get what they want in life. Think about your children's most prized possessions. Are they the ones they worked to earn the money for, or the ones they were given by someone else? There is lifelong value in learning to work hard for the things they want.

Inspection Time

Parents wear many hats, and when it comes to enforcing chores, we often function as both supervisor and quality control inspector. Putting it into those terms takes the emotion out of the equation. Chores are your children's job; you are the supervisor who helps make sure everything gets done, and done well.

Once you assign chores, issue edicts on completion time. That's like lighting a fire under your children's feet. If they can't go play until the work is done, you'll see nothing but a cloud of dust as they race around the house. Before you can blink, you've heard a faint, "'Bye, Mom," as Junior races out the door. Then you go into his room and . . . surprise, the job isn't finished. Or it isn't done right. The bed is made, but all the clothes and toys were shoved underneath, rather than put away. Or the sink and tub were cleaned, but not the toilet. You get the idea. A quickie, halfway job. Not a job well done.

Now what? Avoid the problem before it happens by making sure your children understand that a job isn't finished until it passes inspection. No inspection, no playtime. That means you have to think ahead and make yourself available. And when you do inspect, try to use humor to keep things from getting heated. Also, correct gently. We've often said, "We know you can do a better job than that. You've not given it your best effort. Go ahead and try again, and then I'll come back." When a child does the whole job but leaves out one thing, start with what was done right. Don't just notice the one thing that wasn't up to snuff.

Let me be clear, though: the older the child, the higher the standard. The level of thoroughness required from a five-year-old is light-years from the requirements for a teenager.

I Forgot

Kids, like grown-ups, struggle with both selective hearing and selective memory. They'll forget to feed the dog but clearly remember your promise to take them to the mall. The fact is that we remember the things that are important to us. Kids don't like work, so they won't remember chores unless they have a good reason to. Our job is to give them that reason. We combat this memory loss by withdrawing privileges whenever we hear, "Oops, I forgot."

Our kids have to wash the van and shampoo the dog once every month. We don't care how they divide the work, only that both are clean by the last day of the month. Since nobody likes doing either job, we've had to outlaw complaints and make sure the consequences for forgetting are steep. If the job isn't done by deadline, nobody goes anywhere or does anything until it's finished. No phone, TV, video games, outings with friends. All privileges canceled until the work is done. It's amazing how that has improved their memory.

Some friends of ours prod their kids' memory by charging a did-not-do fine for undone chores, plus requiring the work to be done. Others withdraw a privilege for every incomplete or forgotten chore.

By teaching our children to work and to do a job well, we prepare them to handle future jobs and challenges with confidence. And when they get a "do-over" at home, they also learn to deal with failure, which teaches volumes about persevering and trying again.

Just when you think you have this area covered, be prepared for a spurt when your children act like they've forgotten everything they've ever learned. All of a sudden, lights are left on all over the house, clothes are strewn about, chores don't get done, and your kids act like this is their first day in your house. When this happens, go over the requirements again, and realize that this is a test, though perhaps an unconscious one. The kids want to know, once again, if you mean what you say and if the rules are still the same. Make sure they know that they are.

Laundry 101

When I arrived at college, the number of students—guys and girls—who had no clue how to do laundry blew me away. They had never done it in their lives. Certainly by the time your children are in high school, they should be responsible for their laundry.

Lay the groundwork early, and start kids helping with family laundry. When ours were in elementary school, they learned to put their laundry away. In middle school, they added folding to putting away. Now they're doing their own from start to finish. Things are much less stressful this way. If Princess doesn't have clean socks to wear, whose fault is that? She'll learn. This teaches more than just the basics of sorting by color and choosing water temperature. It requires children to plan ahead and make time in their day or week to take care of this.

Girl vs. Boy Chores

Be careful of dividing chores only along the "traditional" lines. Both boys and girls need to know how to set a proper table, load and unload a dishwasher, and wash and dry dishes. They'll be amazed to learn this doesn't all happen by magic. Children also need to know how to run a vacuum, dust, iron clothes, mop a floor, and clean a toilet. They'll moan and groan about why they need to know all this, but the fact is, no one gets all fired up about cleaning bathrooms, yet bathrooms must be cleaned. They do not magically clean themselves.

Just as guys should know how to do inside chores, girls should know how to pull weeds, sweep or use a blower, trim bushes, operate a weed trimmer, and mow grass. They should also learn basic house and car maintenance.

In today's society, things aren't always divided as they once were. I know one couple in which he cooks and vacuums, while she does the outside chores. Since people often marry later in life, don't buy into the idea that the opposite gender skills are not ones your child will need. "She'll be fine; her husband will mow the yard," isn't smart thinking in today's world. She may not marry. He may not find a wife who'll take over the inside chores. My husband was thirty-eight when we married, and he could iron far better than I could. I still hate ironing, but I know how to do it.

Gardens

Planting a garden is a great thing to do with kids, especially when they're younger. Kids get all fired up about watching things sprout and seeing them grow. Even if you don't have a green thumb—mine is definitely black—plant a few hardy vegetables and nonkillable flowers. It'll be great fun, and your children will learn a lot about responsibility as they care for their plants. The daily discipline of weeding and watering is great training.

Whose Dog Is It, Anyway?

Pets can be a tricky issue. If you have a family pet, all family members should help with its care. For young children, I recommend fish as starter pets, especially since they're generally inexpensive and easy to replace in case of catastrophe. My good friend Leslie Santamaria says her daughter was about five and her son three when two shiny goldfish came to live at their house. The children were so excited and proud of their little fish. Everything was fine until four days later, when one of the little darlings went belly-up right after the children went to bed. *Now what?* the parents wondered. *Do we teach the kids about death and give the fish the traditional "burial at sea" (i.e., flush funeral)?* Finally, just shy of midnight, Leslie's husband snuck out to the local Wal-Mart for a replacement fish, and thankfully, neither of the children was the wiser.

Gerbils and hamsters can be good choices too, but be sure they can't escape. I've heard more than one horror story about gerbils on a rampage chewing a path through boxes of family photos. Land turtles are pretty stress-free pets too, but know at the outset that some of them can live a long, long time.

Don't succumb to pleas for a dog or cat until after your children are old enough to help care for them. My nephew fell in love with our dog at first sight. From that day on, he stopped asking to go see Aunt Connie or Uncle Harry. He begged to see Shadow. One day after his visit, he and his older brother started a "we want a dog" campaign, which my sister-in-law firmly kiboshed, saying, "I already have two children and two cats. The last thing I need is something else to take care of." She's a wise lady. If you get a dog before the kids can take care of it, guess who's going to be out walking Rufus at midnight because "I forgot"?

Depending on the dog's size and weight, kids can start dog-walk patrol when they're seven or eight years old. Be prepared for some funny incidents along the way. Shadow is a forty-five-pound lab mix who can almost pull me off my feet when she gets into four-wheel drive. One day, eight-year-old Ben came in after walking her very upset—and dripping wet. When I asked what was wrong, he said Shadow raced down the hill toward the lake and he couldn't stop her, so she pulled him right into the water with her.

Sure, pets can be messy, annoying, and expensive, but they are also lots of fun and have the added benefit of teaching kids responsibility for something besides themselves and their own needs. Especially at first, you'll have to remind your kids to take care of their pets—over and over and over again. At our house, if we sit down to dinner and Shadow's bowl is empty, we'll ask if she's been fed. If the answer is no, she gets fed immediately—before the people eat. Seeing to her basic needs is part and parcel of our responsibility to her.

Rotating Schedules

To keep our kids from getting frustrated by doing the same chores month after month, we set up a two-week rotating schedule. We post it on the fridge and mark everything on the calendar so there's no mistake. We've been using this plan for several years, and it seems to be working well.

The child doing schedule A takes out the kitchen trash and recycling as needed, takes out all household trash on Saturday (and puts new bags in the trash cans), and washes dishes every day. The child doing schedule B empties the clean dishwasher and drain board, cleans the bathroom once a week, and feeds the dog every morning.

Each child also has weekly chores inside and outside the house to do, plus the monthly van/dog washing. (And when the children want to know—again—why THEY have to wash the van, I remind them—again—just how often that van totes them all over town.)

When the children were younger, we reminded them (they called it nagging) of what had to be done. Now they are expected to live up to their responsibilities without being told. If we're in the middle of a big project or have guests coming, everyone is expected to pitch in and help. Weekly chores aren't the end of their responsibility; they're the bare minimum.

To keep things from getting dragged out way too long, we've set 5:00 p.m. on Saturday as the deadline for chore completion. Otherwise, at 9:00 on Saturday night, we're trying to carry on a conversation above the roar of the vacuum or lawn mower. The children can start their chores earlier in the week, but everything must be done by 5:00 p.m. Saturday. If not, there are consequences, so they'll remember that we're serious and mean what we say.

Car Maintenance and Safety

When your teen starts driving, make sure he or she can change a tire. Yes, there are cell phones today, but what if the phone doesn't work and your teen is stuck? Also, remind your offspring about safety and what to do in an emergency or if they're stranded.

Teach the basics of car maintenance too. There's more to it than putting gas in it once in a while. (As a teen, I was truly shocked when my father started lecturing me about oil changes and tire pressure. Who knew?) Write out a maintenance list, and keep it either in the glove box or in the house. Include instructions and dates to check tire pressure, oil and other fluids, windshield washer fluid and/or antifreeze, and other items. This is an area I admit my husband is clearly the most qualified to oversee, but I know the bare minimum, at least. Make sure your children do too.

The Basics

Make sure your children know how to do simple things like sewing on a button, since something that minor can render a garment unusable. One day, I saw my husband hanging a favorite shirt way, way in the back of the closet. When I asked about it, he said he was putting it in the "do not wear" section. I asked what that was, exactly, and he told me that's where he puts all the clothes waiting for buttons or other repairs. Teach your children how to repair clothes, and eliminate the do-not-wear section.

By the time your sons and daughters leave home, they should also know their way around a stove and microwave and be able to prepare simple meals. When my son said he had no desire to learn to cook, my friend's husband said, "Boy, you need to at least know how to make what you like to eat." Good advice. Assign your children alternating kitchen duty so you can teach them about food prep, how to read recipes, and how to follow instructions on food packages. (As a bonus, you get uninterrupted time to chat.)

Teach your children about recycling. I've often joked that our family recycled long before it became fashionable to do so. When I was a child, tinfoil got reused, and wrapping paper was ironed. Teach good stewardship of the environment. If your town has recycling bins, take younger kids along so they learn about sorting things by category. Pitching cans into the bins can be a fun game.

The Pit (a.k.a. Your Child's Room)

I'm not sure what happens to kids around middle school, but suddenly, not only are their bedrooms a mess, they smell like a locker room too. It probably has a little something to do with that puberty/hormone thing. Every parent I've talked to is frustrated by this lack of respect for stuff and complete disregard for order. If this rings any bells, hang tough. You are not alone.

First, decide what level of mess you're willing to tolerate. (This is part of that "choose your battles" thing.) Every family will handle this issue differently. I know many parents who simply turn a blind eye. Others hound and nag and ground the children until the room is clean. Go with whatever approach works for you. We decided clothing was too expensive to be crumpled underfoot, so clothes on the floor is strictly verboten at our house. If clothing is found on the floor, the culprit—whether child or adult—must pay a per-item charge into the family money jar. (We empty the jar on vacation and use the money to go out to dinner.) At first, the cost was ten cents per item, but that had no effect since the price wasn't high enough to hurt. So we raised it until we got results.

As for keeping the room clean, we decided it had to meet the Saturday-at-five deadline. If it was a pigsty the rest of the week, we'd close the door as we went by, but it had to be clean once a week. Also, Friday-night sleepovers don't happen until the room is clean and weekly chores are done. We heard the "But we didn't have time" excuse too many times. Here again, set the rules ahead of time, so kids know what to expect. You'd be amazed at how motivated your daughter will get if she knows (a) Becky can't come over until I finish, or (b) I can't go to Becky's sleepover unless I finish. And if the job isn't done right, she won't go at all. Be sure to offer praise for a job well done.

Miscellaneous Stuff

Stray junk was a much bigger problem when our children were younger. Seems everywhere they went, they left a trail of clothing and toys, so we made a game out of seeing how much stuff we could put away before the timer rang. When they got older and saw through that little "game," we started collecting things left lying around in a laundry basket. Shoes? Homework? Jacket? We charged a fee to get them back. It's amazing what a great motivator money can be.

Inventory Reduction

Have you noticed the self-storage units popping up like wild mushrooms everywhere you turn? Friends, if we have to pay to keep all of our belongings under roof, we have too many of them.

I wish I could say I have this area under control, but as anyone who's seen my office can tell you, it's not true. It's hard to admonish my children to get rid of their junk when I have to step over piles of my own. My husband and I are both pack rats, and since pack rats tend to raise pack rats, this is a challenge for our family. But we're getting better.

The reality is simple: we're not taking it with us. Our souls will not be whisked off to heaven clutching our favorite possessions. The things we'll have in heaven are the ones we've sent on ahead, the things that "moth and rust do not destroy, and where thieves do not break in and steal" (Matt. 6:20). After we're gone, most of our stuff will end up in a yard sale or thrift store. Why, then, do we hang on so tightly?

I think some of it is a simple case of the "covets." Constant media bombardment and the sensory overload of superstores convince us we gotta have it all and gotta have it now. We can walk into the mall perfectly content and walk out totally dissatisfied. Sometimes it's better to stay home.

In our consumer-oriented society, how do we teach our children the proper perspective on possessions? The same way they learn most things: by example. (Nobody said it would be easy.)

If something no longer serves a purpose in your life, let it go. Who says you can't give family heirlooms as gifts? (This saves money too, and it offers the recipient something meaningful.) Speaker Gaye Martin tells how her aunt approached this thinning-out process. Whenever she bequeathed an item, she would tell the recipient, "I've enjoyed this piece, but now I think it's time for it to come and live at your house."

Another way is to hold an annual "inventory reduction sale" (i.e., yard sale). Or donate unused items to your church or a local charity. You can take a tax deduction if you keep a record of what you've given. Do whatever you must to loosen your hold on things.

Last year, our old console TV started gasping and coughing. It was definitely the death rattle. The kids wanted a big, new TV, but since that wasn't in the budget, we told them we'd have a yard sale. The amount we earned would determine the size of the screen. We all sorted through our junk and now have less cluttered closets and a very nice new TV set.

The One-In-One-Out Method

Admittedly, my family has not mastered this one, but we're trying. If a new appliance comes in, the old one should go out. Trash broken things and donate working ones. Keeping duplicates is hoarding.

Before or immediately after your children's birthdays or Christmas, help them go through their stuff and sort out what they don't need any longer. Simply buying or building more shelf space to hold more stuff is not the answer.

If we truly believe that God will supply all our needs, let's model that for our children. Get rid of unnecessary extras, and teach your children to do the same.

I spent six weeks in the Philippines during college, and it forever changed my perspective. I would love to take all the teenagers I know to an emerging nation so they could appreciate all that they have. Most of the world does not live like Americans do. We have so much and don't even realize it. I saw whole families living in cardboard huts the size of refrigerator boxes. Imagine my shock when they invited me in to share what little food they had.

We have been blessed with more than we need. Let's be good stewards of the bounty God placed in our hands. And let's teach our children to do the same.

So as you think about teaching your children life skills, ask yourself these questions:

- Do my children have daily and weekly household responsibilities? Are these posted clearly?
- Are there clear consequences for not doing chores? Am I consistent in enforcing them?
- Have I set standards for the children's rooms?
- Am I teaching my children—by example—to hold their possessions with an open hand?
- Do we regularly clear out our extra stuff?
- Who cares for the family pet(s)?
- How do I cure selective memory at our house?

If you have late elementary/middle school children:

- Are my children involved in doing the laundry, from elementary school on up?
- Am I teaching both my sons and my daughters how to wash dishes, run a vacuum, dust, iron, and clean a bathroom?
- Can my children do basics like sew on a button?
- Have I taught them the safe operation of household appliances?

- Have I made sure my children know lawn and garden basics like weeding and watering, mowing a lawn, and raking leaves?
- Do I regularly inspect my children's work—before they leave the house?
- How do I handle miscellaneous junk left lying around?

If you have older teens:

- Are my teens responsible for their laundry?
- Do I involve my teens in meal preparation?
- Can they read recipes and cook simple foods?
- Once my children start driving, have I taught them how to change a tire? What to do in an emergency? Basic car maintenance?
- Do I assign do-overs for less than stellar work?
- What are the consequences for "Oops, I forgot"? Are they clearly defined?

5

Values

In the aftermath of the hurricanes that hit Florida in 2004, generators instantly became the most sought-after and precious of commodities. If you were fortunate enough to have one, you considered yourself blessed and offered fridge space or a cooling-off spot to your neighbors. If you didn't, honest people sipped tepid water and prayed for power restoration. Others, though, decided they were entitled to a generator, no matter whose it was.

One man went to bed, relieved that his generator had enough power to run his ceiling fans and provide some relief from the suffocating heat. Sometime during the night he woke up, drenched in sweat. He listened. Yep, he could still hear the generator, but the fans weren't spinning. When he went outside to investigate, he discovered that someone had stolen his generator and put a running lawn mower in its place so the lack of generator noise wouldn't alert him.

As a parent, I have to wonder if the thief had children and how he or she explained the sudden appearance of a generator. A lie, perhaps?

Since values are one of the most important and foundational traits our children need to internalize and make their own, how can we teach values to our children? Illustrations like this one are a great tool, but the number-one way your children will learn values is by watching you. How you live—your priorities, how you spend your time and money, how you treat others and your possessions—is the single best indicator of what matters to you and what values you hold dear. Believe me, your children read your life far more clearly than they heed your words. If both are in harmony, that's great. If they're not, look out. It's time to reevaluate.

Critical Thinking

In today's world, critical thinking is a vital skill our children must learn. I don't mean teaching them to be critical; I mean teaching them to analyze what they see, hear, and read so they can make good judgments and sound decisions.

For example, when the science teacher tells your fourth grader that we descended from apes, what will your child say? Both of ours came home and told us they'd heard the funniest thing in school: the teacher thought people came from monkeys.

It is vital that we tell our children how our views and values fly in the face of what's being taught in the world today. Dinnertime is a great time to reconnect and to discuss what's happening in school and in the world around us. At our house, we've started a regular dinnertime feature we call "News of the Absurd." My husband shares tidbits gleaned from talk radio that show just how mixed-up and crazy people's thinking has gotten. A classic example was the news that a group of people planned to sue several fast-food chains for making them fat.

Stories like these give us an opportunity to talk about personal responsibility and the consequences of our actions and choices. However, we never want this to be a one-sided conversation, where we lecture and the children stir the food around on their plates. We have told them that questions are always OK, as long as they're asked respectfully. We want our kids to say, "What do you mean by that? Why are we against thus-and-so?"

Young children take our beliefs and opinions at face value, but as they get older, they have to make those beliefs their own. One of the ways they do that is by questioning what they've been taught. That process panics many parents. Don't let it.

Sometimes our kids ask a question and we say, "Let us do some more research, because right now, we can't give you a good answer." That usually means they've questioned something we haven't clearly thought through ourselves. We make finding an answer a priority, because getting back to them in a timely manner says we are taking their questions seriously. If we forget, rest assured they won't, and they'll perceive the lack of response as disinterest in what matters to them. As they get older, we also encourage them to do some research on their own. Then we get together, usually over dinner, and discuss our findings. This has led to some fascinating discussions and glimpses into what issues and questions matter to them.

Other times, they'll give us their opinion, and we'll carefully ask questions, sometimes to gently point out the flaws in their logic and thinking, sometimes to give them a chance to think things through. We want to provide a safe environment where our kids can process their thoughts and gradually internalize what they've been taught.

Store clerks and bank tellers learn to recognize counterfeit money by handling the real thing. They say the fake stuff just doesn't feel the same. Truth is a lot like that. If you teach your children biblical truth from the time they are young, it will be much easier for them to recognize falsehood when someone tries to convince them of it.

For example, our children were still in elementary school when we started telling them why we believe abstinence is the only logical, safe, God-approved choice before marriage. We wanted them prepared when they studied sex education in school. Even if your kids roll their eyes when you bring up these subjects, don't despair; they are listening. We want our children to know exactly where we stand on every one of society's "hot-button" issues, so they'll be able to respond intelligently when the topics come up at school or with friends. We don't want them left wondering what we think or how they should respond.

Our son was about ten years old when friends tried to talk him into playing Dungeons and Dragons. He watched for a while, but when they invited him to join in, he said no. We'd never discussed this particular game with him, but he said the whole thing seemed off in some way he couldn't put his finger on, so he didn't play. We then explained some of the concerns parents have about the game (including the desensitizing aspects of role-playing evil characters and the game's occultic overtones) and how proud we were of him.

Discernment is a wonderful gift and important skill that we give our children by building a foundation of biblical truth into their lives. Later, when other ideas and philosophies cross their path, they can hold those ideas up to the truth they know and determine whether or not these things fit what they know to be true.

The New Tolerance

Critical thinking and discernment are essential for combating a mind-set that is sweeping our culture and affecting how both Christians and non-Christians view the world. Josh McDowell calls this shift in thinking "The New Tolerance," and he's written a book by the same title. I recommend you grab a copy. The concepts seem simple enough on the surface, but the implications are chilling.

If your child attends public school—possibly even private school—you've seen handouts and rules about tolerance. Now on the surface, this seems like a fine idea, one we all grew up believing: we must show respect for others' opinions and beliefs. However, that isn't what tolerance means in today's world. The new tolerance says that ALL values, beliefs, lifestyles, and truth claims are equal. None is better than any others, and therefore there is no right or wrong. The only important thing is what I believe.[1]

Read that again. Frightening, isn't it? Absolutes? Gone. Right or wrong? Doesn't exist. But even that is not enough. The new tolerance says that to be truly tolerant, we must not only accept others' definition of truth, but we must support their beliefs and behaviors.

This is a radical departure from the way things have been for centuries. Up until now, Western civilization followed what's called "ethical theism," which holds that there are absolutes of right and wrong that were decided by God and communicated to us. Today's postmodern culture says that objective truth doesn't exist. There are no absolutes; experience dictates the standard. When a college professor asks his students if the Holocaust was wrong and the students respond that they can't say for sure, we have a huge problem with our thinking.[2]

Those who believe in God and follow his guidelines—like the Ten Commandments—do believe that there is right and wrong and that the standard applies equally to everyone. God set out clear thou-shalt-nots; choosing to ignore and disbelieve them doesn't change the standard. The yardstick hasn't disappeared just because people don't want to measure their lives by it.

In a culture that teaches all beliefs are OK—except, of course, ones that promote absolutes—how do we raise children with godly values? We start by refuting the absurdity of the new tolerance. With this belief, Hitler's actions can't be condemned as evil, because no one can make moral judgments. Maybe we can't, but God can—and does. He says murder is wrong.

The new tolerance also says that you can't separate people from their actions. Of course you can. We do it all the time. So does God. He loves sinners even as he condemns our sin. I often tell my children that I love them dearly, but I am not impressed with a particular behavior, and it must stop.

To love someone does not mean I must love everything he or she does. The two are not the same. A dear friend has embraced the gay lifestyle. My affection for him and the value I place on our friendship has not changed, though my heart grieves the choices he's made. In the same way, if a family member made some poor choices, perhaps even committed a horrible crime, we would still love the person, while condemning his or her choices. How Christ dealt with people during his earthly ministry provides the example for us.

I do want to be careful and emphasize that condemning someone's actions does not mean teaching your children to be obnoxious and self-righteous, loudly pointing out the sins of others. The Bible has a great deal to say about judging. It also talks about getting the beams out of our own eyes before we point out the specks in others' eyes (Matt. 7:3–5).

My point is that we need to expose this new tolerance for the lie that it is and teach our children to recognize it so it doesn't slip into their thinking. We must model Christ's example of gently loving others without condoning their misdeeds and poor choices. We must teach our children what we believe and help them find ways to politely, calmly defend those beliefs when challenged.

Second, we must teach our children the attributes and attitudes the Bible promotes, starting with loving others as we love ourselves. That means we condemn the belief, not the person. Christ told the truth, tempered with love.

One of the results of new-tolerance thinking is the idea that parents have no "right" to tell children what to do; rather, children should make their own choices. Eventually they will, but until they are grown and on their own, parents make the rules. Respecting parental standards, and the parents themselves, is not optional, regardless of this new thinking. God set up the family the way he wanted it. Make sure your children understand that.

Last, especially as your children reach the teen years, help them deal with this shift in collective worldview by encouraging honest discussion and questions. This gives them an opportunity to verbalize their beliefs and us an opportunity to help shape their worldview by guiding them toward God's absolute truth. Ask questions to start the conversational ball rolling: "What happens to society if there is no right or wrong? What happens to our laws? If Jesus is the Way, can other ways also lead to heaven? How can we separate a person's beliefs from his or her actions?"

Former secretary of education William J. Bennett had this to say about moral education and children:

> Some educators deliberately avoid questions of right and wrong or remain neutral about them. Many have turned to values education theories that seek to guide children in developing their own values by discussion, dialogue and simulation—a tragic approach, since research indicates it has no discernable effect on children's behavior. At best, this misguided method threatens to leave our children morally adrift.[3]

In the years since, we've seen evidence of the truth of this statement in public policy and practical application. We played a card game with several children one night and explained that if you couldn't play a card, you had to say "pass." Later, we found that one of the girls had been "passing" in order to avoid playing certain cards. When we told her that was cheating, she said, "But you didn't tell me I couldn't."

We must teach our children the basics of right and wrong. If postmodernism and the new tolerance are not concepts you've thought much about, take time to do that and to formulate your position. Read Josh McDowell's book, and check out the Barna Group's website (http://www.barna.org) for statistics and family resources and the Focus on the Family website (http://www.family.org) for more information. Then talk with your children. Help them examine what they're being taught in light of the truth of God's Word so they can formulate a solid view from which to see the world.

Kindness and Compassion

These values seem to have gone the way of eight-track tapes and vinyl albums. They're still around, but they're harder to come by and viewed as quaint. If you study the media, politics, or celebrities, trash talking and put-downs have become commonplace. While the new tolerance says people and their actions are tied together and must all be valued, there seems to be no end to the insult slinging. One look at the latest reality-TV offerings proves America can't get enough of seeing others lied to, misled, insulted, embarrassed, injured, manipulated, or otherwise mistreated. Hollywood wouldn't keep offering these programs if people didn't watch.

By the time kids hit middle school, they're starting to pull away from their parents a bit, working to establish an identity separate from their parents. Too often, put-downs become a way for them to feel better about themselves. I admit I was guilty of it too. By age fourteen, I'd hit my full height of 5 feet, 1½ inches, early in the morning if I stood up real straight. After I'd heard every short joke known to man, I got tired of it. I started deflecting the jabs with ones of my own. Actually, I became quite proud of my reputation as "queen of the put-down"—this from a girl who spent her summers on mission trips and was trying to live a Christlike life. Several years later, a youth pastor pointed out the discrepancy in my life and forced me to reconsider.

Though the memory chafes, it reminds me how compartmentalized teens can be in their thinking. I was one person at school and someone else at church. If you've had similar experiences, share them with your teens. Make them understand that character is who you are when you're all alone and there's no one to see you.

Teaser and Teased

Children rarely get through the growing-up years without being both the one being picked on and the one taking jabs at others. As parents, it's our job to come down hard when the latter occurs. Put-downs aren't right, and it's our job to say so. If you discover your child has hurt someone verbally, make sure he apologizes. He'll protest long and loud and offer rafts of excuses about how the other person started it, it wasn't his fault, and so on. Stand firm. If he won't apologize, raise the stakes until apologizing looks better than the alternative. To apologize means to swallow your pride and admit you were wrong. No one likes to do this, but it's a skill we must learn. Let your children see you do it when needed, and assure them that eating crow isn't fatal, merely uncomfortable.

When your child is on the receiving end of trash talk, use it as an opportunity to offer comfort but also to teach a lesson in empathy. "This feels really awful, doesn't it? Remember this feeling and how much it hurts the next time you're tempted to pick on someone else. What you're feeling right now is how others feel when you pick on them."

As children get older, put-downs get excused with, "But I was only teasing." Ugly jokes that poke fun are not OK. As parents, it's our responsibility to say, "You've crossed the line. Apologize and back way up on that issue." Remind your children that even if the other person laughed, he or she is probably hiding the hurt behind a smile—just as they've done when someone made fun of them.

I recently heard about a middle school boy who has become a target of ridicule. He is extremely polite, very smart, a teensy bit slow of speech, and very big physically. Every day when he boards the school bus, most of the seats are already taken, so he asks the same boy if he can share a seat with him. And every day, the other boy shouts, "No way! Get away, you freak!" But this boy keeps asking, very politely, day after day after day. I want to cry when I picture this boy walking home every day wondering why no one is nice to him. I was relieved to hear that at least one child on the bus defends him, telling the other children to be nice and stop being mean.

The Golden Rule is a biblical concept. Teach it—and live it. Let your children see you treat others the way you want to be treated. If we don't set the standards in our homes, our children won't learn right behavior elsewhere. They won't in our "tolerant" society. The job is ours. Show that people matter. The way you treat others—from good friends and family to the clerk at the store—will show your children whether you live what you believe.

Work Is Good

Charles J. Sykes, author of *Dumbing Down Our Kids*, compiled a list of rules kids won't learn in school. Among the rules are, "You will not make $40,000 a year right out of high school. You won't be a vice president with a car phone until you 'earn' both."[4] Yet many kids expect exactly that. They're in for a rude awakening. I've talked with teens who don't want a job washing dishes or busing tables because they think that's beneath them. "I ain't gonna do that. I'm better than that. I'm gonna get me a real job." Six months later, they're still sitting home watching soap operas and playing video games.

Speaker Gaye Martin does lots of corporate training and says she's amazed at how often she's asked to speak on punctuality. It's becoming a huge problem for companies. Employees regularly show up thirty minutes late for work and don't see it as an issue. When confronted with this, many shrug and say, "I'm not a morning person."

If we want our children to succeed in the workforce, we will teach them that punctuality and getting the job done on time go along with hard work. As a child, I wanted to go play and forget about work. But my mother knew what I did not. Getting the work done first kept me from having a black cloud hanging over my head the whole day. The desire to procrastinate—especially on tasks we really don't want to do—is common to almost everyone. By teaching our children how great it feels to get the hard stuff over with and then be free to play, we pass on another important life skill and attitude.

Honesty and Integrity

These two increasingly rare qualities go hand in hand. Integrity means being honest in your dealings with others and doing what you say you will do. Lack of it is one of the reasons long legal contracts have replaced a handshake to seal a business deal. Live in such a way that people know you mean what you say and your word can be counted on. If your child gets invited to a party and commits to going, don't let her weasel out if a better offer comes along later. The same applies to dates for the prom or other events.

Have you taught your children that lying is always wrong? We've made it clear that if our kids lie to cover up some misdeed, the consequences will be far greater than if they'd 'fessed up to begin with. Honesty is still and always the best policy.

Some argue that polite societal lies are okay. No, they're not. Your children watch you every minute of every day. If someone you don't wish to speak with calls your house and you instruct your children to say you're not home, you're teaching that it's OK to lie. If they overhear you tell someone you can't come over because you have thus-and-such to do, and then you tell your children you just didn't feel like going, you're teaching them to lie.

Usually we lie because we don't want to look bad. It's as simple as that. But integrity and maturity mean taking responsibility for our actions and owning up when we mess up. If we teach our children that compromising the little things is OK, we shouldn't be surprised if they see "big" compromises as OK later.

Make sure your children understand that it is unacceptable to take anything that doesn't belong to them or that they don't have permission to take. That applies to stores, restaurants, people's homes, the church kitchen, and even their siblings' rooms. If you catch them stealing, assign a consequence so memorable they won't be tempted to do it again. Ever.

Recently we heard about a man who spent twenty years working for a manufacturing company. He got fired for stealing scrap metal. What he stole was worth less than $150, but taking it cost him his job and his reputation.

Teach your children early that it is not only wrong to cheat on a test, it's also wrong to let others steal answers from them. Encourage your children to stand firm against peer pressure in this area.

Integrity even comes into play in situations I always thought went without saying. Plagiarism is becoming a huge problem in schools, especially with all the handy information available on the Internet. One teacher I know prints out papers from popular websites so she can compare them to what her students turn in. She was amazed at how many simply cut and paste info into their papers without a qualm—or a footnote. Copying material without giving credit to the source is stealing.

Kids often lie to see how much they can get away with. If you come down with both feet, they'll understand what you expect. Sometimes *Not Me* shows up to claim responsibility for broken vases, shattered windows, and misplaced toys. If your children start this, look them in the eyes and go with your instincts. Body language often gives them away, and sometimes you know there's more to it than you're getting. If we can't figure out who did it, and neither of our children will confess, we have to make a judgment call. Either they both get punished, or we go with our gut and mete out discipline to the one we believe is guilty. We may be wrong sometimes, but I don't think it's very often. You know your kids. Trust your gut.

Model and teach integrity early. Make sure your children understand that these values encompass every area of life. Little things do matter. Reputation is important.

Teach them to stand up for what's right. Be sure you applaud them when they do, because outside your home, doing the right thing may well earn them ridicule and scorn.

As you try to instill good values in your children, ask yourself:

- Can I articulate what my family's standards and values are? If not, spend some time doing so.
- Can my children tell truth from lies?
- Have I taught my children that there are absolutes of right and wrong? How?
- Have I shown them clearly the fallacy of the new tolerance and helped them see the faulty thinking that lies beneath it?
- Have I taught them how to politely disagree when someone accuses them of being narrow-minded or old-fashioned because they believe in right and wrong?
- Have I taught them that there is a difference between who a person is and what a person does?
- Have I taught them to show love and compassion to others?
- Do my children hear me utter polite lies to save face?
- Does the way I live model honesty and integrity?
- Do I pay my taxes, or do I hide extra income?
- Do I treat others the way I want to be treated?
- Do I give my boss my all on the job, or do I do as little as possible?

If you have late elementary/middle school children:

- Have I made my children apologize if they've hurt someone's feelings?
- Have they seen and heard me do the same?
- Do my children know that stealing is wrong?
- What are the consequences for lying?
- Is doing my best important to me? How do I model that for my children?
- Do I require my children to do their best on everything, be it chores, schoolwork, or sports?

If you have older teens:

- Do my teens know what the family standards and values are?
- Can they articulate those values to others?
- Have we role-played specific conversations or scenarios to help my teens calmly refute "new tolerance" thinking?
- Do I require my teens to stick to commitments they've made—even if a better offer comes along?
- Do my teens know, through practice at home, how to work and give it their all?
- Do my teens understand that punctuality matters?
- Have I let my teens know that put-downs are unacceptable behavior?

6

Talents, Gifts, Acceptance, and Communication

The story made headlines. Two young sisters were playing in the driveway of their suburban home, their dolls set up in the shadow of the family station wagon. Without warning, laughter turned to terror when the car's emergency brake failed and the vehicle rolled down the drive. The girls scrambled to get out of the way, but they weren't quite quick enough. When the car finally rolled to a stop, the youngest sister was pinned beneath the rear tire.

Alerted by the screaming, their mother raced out the front door, her horrified eyes taking in the scene at a glance. "Call the police," she shouted to her older daughter; then she raced to the car.

Neighbors rushed outside at the commotion, and when they reached the scene, they couldn't believe their eyes.

The mother, barely five feet tall, stood at the back of the car, chrome bumper gripped in her hands, teeth gritted as she lifted the car off her daughter.

Frantic hands reached in to help, and by the time the police and fire rescue arrived, the little girl had already been pulled from beneath the car. She was hospitalized overnight and then returned to her mother's waiting arms.

Do your children know that in similar circumstances, you would do the same for them? Do they feel you love them—just the way they are? Do you know what unique gifts and talents God has given them? Sometimes we're so busy rushing from one activity to another that we don't think about these things and don't take the time to make sure our children know how important they are to us.

It is critical that we take time to listen to our children's hearts, to hear the dreams God has planted deep inside them. My dream to write books was born while I read *Little Women*, *Lassie*, and *Harriet the Spy*, but I didn't have the courage to pursue my dream until many years later. The spark was always there, though, waiting to be fanned into flame.

Encourage Creativity and Self-Entertainment

Every person has a unique personality, interests, talents, and dreams. Watch how your children spend their time for clues as to how God wired them. Limit access to the "boob tube," and you'll give them opportunities to discover and develop their talents. I'm not saying you should pitch your TV onto the front lawn, though that wouldn't hurt, but the TV should never be used simply as background noise.

When we moved from bustling Fort Lauderdale, Florida, to a small town in central Florida, we decided to forgo cable TV. We didn't want our children forever glued to the tube, and we didn't want to be that way either. For a while, the kids groaned, because we only got three channels—four if wind direction and barometric pressure were just right. But getting rid of cable did wonders for the kids' creativity. Because there were so few programs that came in clearly, they did other things instead. We recently installed a big antenna, and now we have to be careful again. It's too easy to get sucked in for several mindless hours. Be conscious of what you're doing. Watch a specific program, and then turn the thing off. Listen to the radio or CDs instead if you want background sound.

Be careful of video and computer games too. Yes, some of them can teach certain skills, but they don't require the same imagination and creativity that unstructured playtime does. Simply tell your children to go find something to do. As they get older, they'll look you in the eye and tell you there isn't anything to do. They're bored and need to go to the mall. At that point, our standard response is, "If you can't find something to do, I'll get my list. Weeds need to be pulled, the car needs to be washed. . . ." Usually, before I finish rattling off options, they're out the door, because they've just remembered several things they could do.

We set the stage for creativity and self-entertainment when our children were toddlers. I regularly announced that it was time for them to go play in their rooms for a while. I'd peek in occasionally to see what they were up to and then wait for them to come out. Usually one hour, maybe two, would go by before they reemerged. They'd play with Legos, blocks, cars, or dolls, or they'd read, color, or draw. They'd come up with all kinds of creative things.

The trick, though, is to provide children with the time to explore and create. If you're always running somewhere, your children never get that opportunity. Help them develop the skill of entertaining themselves and discover the joy of creativity.

They will also need creativity tools. For elementary age children, get a plastic tub and stock it with Popsicle sticks, glue, glitter, Play-Doh, cotton balls, dried pasta, empty paper towel rolls, string, or whatever you can think of. You'll be amazed at how much fun they'll have and what they'll build and create.

Some children love to draw and color, others love to read, and still others are happiest when they're involved in sports, music, drama, or working with their hands in some way. Find those activities that make your children's eyes light up and make them quiver with excitement.

Understand that as they grow, their interests will change and change rapidly. That's OK. We usually don't invest a lot of money in the most recent interest until we've seen whether it will last or not. If your daughter expresses an interest in making beaded jewelry, start with one small kit or a few supplies. If those get used and she's begging for more, then get more. But don't stock a closet full of beads and wire the first time she mentions it. Let your children try different things without pressure.

Failure as a Tool

As your children try new things, they will occasionally fail. That's OK too. Failure is a part of life, and if we don't allow them the opportunity to fall once in a while, how will they learn to get back up and try again? Remember learning to ride a bike? Sew? Drive? None of it was accomplished on the first try. Don't shield your children from failure. Encourage them to step out and try new things. If it doesn't work, encourage them to dust themselves off and try again. That's how we learn.

John Rosemond says failure "lets the child come to grips with the frustration inherent to the learning of any skill—social, academic, emotional and so on. That's how children learn to persevere, and perseverance—as we all know from experience—is the main ingredient in every success story."[1] Every time a child tries, fails, and then tries again, he or she builds confidence. Don't rob your children of this important skill. In this case, help by not helping.

Rosemond advises offering empathy, rather than sympathy. "Empathy involves understanding, and sends the message, 'What are you going to do about it?' Sympathy, on the other hand, involves pampering and sends the message, 'Oh, you poor thing! You haven't done anything to deserve this!'"[2]

Help your children learn to solve their own problems. I am learning to bite my tongue when confronted with a request for help. Instead of spewing solutions and options all over my offspring, I'm trying to take a deep breath and instead ask them how they plan to work this out. It's been working wonders for their confidence level—and my frustration level.

Who Are You?

We've had some fun at our house with various personality analysis tests. We have discovered that our family contains both introverts and extroverts. We have highly creative types and strongly analytical types and every possible combination of both.

Remind your children that they do not have to be like anybody else, because God made each of them unique. Our son can draw fabulous pictures, while Harry's and my stick figures look silly. Our daughter can whip out a wonderful poem in ten minutes, while I couldn't come up with a single rhyming phrase in an hour and a half.

Celebrate Your Child's Uniqueness

Recently our family had a wonderful time at the dinner table talking about Gary Chapman's book *The Five Love Languages*. In it, he says that we all perceive love in one primary way. People feel most loved when those around them express that love in the way that meets their deepest needs. He defines the five love languages as (1) words of affirmation, (2) quality time, (3) receiving gifts, (4) acts of service, and (5) physical touch.[3] This was an eye-opener for me, because I realized my love language is quality time, with gifts as number two. I feel loved when those I love want to spend time with me. But this is not the primary language of the others in my family. We realized that we love each other best when we show love to the other family members in the way that's most meaningful to them.

What about your family? Talk about how you perceive love. If you're not sure which language is primary for family members, watch how they show love to others. We often express love in the way we want to receive it.

Is your home populated by lions, beavers, otters, or golden retrievers? This is how Gary Smalley and John

Trent classify the four personality types in their book *The Two Sides of Love.* Other personality tests group people by color or primary attribute, but amazingly, the results are usually pretty consistent from test to test. Grab a copy of a personality profile, and then spend an evening working through it together. You'll have a great time learning about each other and how we see ourselves versus how others see us.

Thank God for making you all so different, and help your children maximize the positives and deal with the negatives of their personality type. Especially as they go through the turbulent, identity-questioning teen years, show love and acceptance for who they are, right then. Get excited about the talents and gifts God's given them, and celebrate the unique traits with which he's blessed them.

A bitter pill for parents to swallow is the disappointment of a child whose interests and abilities are nothing like theirs. Beware of the message you send. An athletic, sports-oriented dad whose son prefers art and music has a choice to make. Dad can encourage and accept his son's uniqueness, or he can try to mold the boy into what he wants him to be. Option two will be frustrating and discouraging for both of them. Try to find common ground and celebrate the gifts and interests God has given each of you. He made your children exactly the people he wants them to be, uniquely designed for the work and ministry he has planned for them.

Our son found soccer, loved it, and has been playing for seven years. Our daughter has had fun trying different things: she's played T-ball and softball, taken gymnastics, played soccer, and, most recently, is learning to play the guitar, which she loves. It's OK to experiment. If your kids show an interest, encourage it. If they absolutely hate the sport or activity they chose, that's fine. When the time commitment has been met, chalk it up to experience, and encourage them to try something else.

Communication Is Key

Kids talk when they know someone will listen. If you only give them half your attention, they'll know and will think twice about coming to you again. Stop what you're doing, and look them in the eyes. If you really can't listen right then, set a time to talk and then stick to it. That lets your children know they matter to you.

Don't nag for the sake of nagging. Correction may be necessary, but remember that when someone says several nice things and one not-so-nice, the negative is remembered first. Therefore, balance requirements with acceptance and love. If all you do is criticize, your children will avoid you, but if you provide an atmosphere of acceptance and love, they'll tell you what's on their minds.

Sometimes you need to create the opportunity for good conversation. I've found that the best time is when one of the kids and I are driving somewhere. They ask amazing questions and tell me things they wouldn't during the normal hustle and bustle. Schedule times like that. Create opportunities to talk. Active listening is a tangible way to show love to our kids.

Carefully guard your children's privacy, and be sure you don't blab things they tell you in confidence. As they get into the teen years, assume everything is confidential unless they tell you otherwise. Teens are very private. How well you protect that privacy will determine how much information they give you. (Keeping confidences doesn't mean situations of danger to the child or a friend or keeping secrets from your spouse. This means generalized lip flapping.)

Be Your Child's Cheerleader

Know this: children get fired up if they feel their interests and activities are important to you. Get involved in whatever your child is involved in. At the very least, be there. I was speechless when I realized how many children played on sports teams but had parents who didn't attend a single game! That's terrible. It broke my heart to watch kids scan the audience week after week, hoping for a parental face. We did our best to encourage them, but it's not the same as when the praise and support comes from mom and dad. Be there for your kids. Show them that their interests matter to you. When our kids were in elementary school, they wanted us to see every practice, plus the games. Now that they're older, they'd prefer we not watch practice, but my husband and I make sure at least one of us—if not both—is at every game. Parents, your presence matters to your kids. Show them that their interests matter to you as well. Show up—rain or shine, convenient or not.

Also, remind your children that the gifts and talents they've been given are not just for their benefit. Help your children figure out how they can use their talents to help others. If your child excels at sports, teach him to be an encourager on the team, to be the one trying to help those not as advanced, instead of poking fun at the "athletically challenged." If your child is into art of some kind, encourage her to give pieces away or to display them where they will brighten others' lives. If he's into music, have him sing or play at church. Gifts are to be used, not hoarded. Teach your children ways to do that.

As you teach your children about gifts and talents, ask yourself:

- Do I know what my children's unique gifts and abilities are?
- How am I encouraging my children to develop their gifts further?
- What are my gifts?
- How am I using them?
- How involved am I in what interests my children?
- When was the last time I attended a game, asked to see a drawing, or read a story to my child?
- Am I requiring my children to be involved in the things I want, or am I allowing them to choose activities that appeal to their interests and abilities?
- In what practical ways am I encouraging their interests?

If you have late elementary/middle school children:

- Do I send my children to find something to do besides TV or video games?
- Have I provided creativity supplies?
- What is my child's primary love language?
- What is my child's personality type?
- Do I know my child's dreams?

If you have older teens:

- Does my teen know I love who he or she is today?
- Do I make sure I balance correction with love?
- When was the last time I spent uninterrupted time with my teen?
- Do I know what's on my teen's mind and what issues are most important to him or her?
- Do I show acceptance for my child, even when the behavior must be modified?
- How am I encouraging my teen to use his or her gifts?

7

Spirituality

George Barna and the Barna Research Group con-
ducted several studies regarding the age at which
people come to Christ. Among their findings was the
fact that the probability of someone embracing Christ
as Savior drops from 32 percent to 4 percent between
ages 13 and 18.[1] "Given the trends indicating that your
spiritual condition by the age of 13 is a strong predictor
of your spiritual profile as an adult, it seems clear that
a deep and robust spiritual life demands intentional and
strategic spiritual nurturing during the early childhood
and adolescent years."[2]

These numbers remind us of the importance of instilling our faith in our children from the very beginning. If
we teach our children all of the practical life skills but
neglect their spiritual education, we've left out the heart
of the matter. Humans are born with a hunger to under-

stand and a desire to know that there is a Creator who has things under control—especially when things in this world make no sense.

Mismatched Faith?

What if you and your spouse come from different spiritual backgrounds? Some parents in this situation say, "We're not going to force our beliefs on our children. We'll let them choose later when they're adults." By that time, frankly, it's too late. You can't sprinkle spirituality into their lives as an afterthought. The time to train your children spiritually is when they're young. Even if you and your spouse come from different faiths, find a way to teach your children what you believe, stressing the areas where both faiths agree.

Saying nothing is the worst possible choice. Ultimately, every person will have to make a choice about his or her relationship with God and with God's Son, Jesus Christ. Seek wisdom and creative, peaceful ways to deal with the two-faith issue in your home, but don't deprive your children of their spiritual heritage.

Let the Church Teach 'Em

Even if you and your spouse share the same faith background, don't assume you've done your job if you drop the children off at church while you go out for brunch. That merely teaches children that church isn't important for grown-ups. Fellowship in a church is vital—for all family members.

The Bible gives some clear directives for parents in Deuteronomy 6:6–7: "These commandments that I give you today are to be upon your hearts. Impress them on your children. Talk about them when you sit at home and when you walk along the road, when you lie down and when you get up."

This reminds us that spiritual training is not just a Sunday-morning activity and that the responsibility isn't the Sunday school teachers'. It's our job to instill our beliefs in our children. Proverbs 22:6 says to "train up a child in the way he should go: and when he is old, he will not depart from it" (KJV). The habits and beliefs we instill when our children are young are the ones they'll remember later.

Evaluate Your Beliefs

We each have our own relationship with God, so our children can't hitch a ride on our faith. Someday God will ask us about our relationship to him, and he'll ask our children the same question. Our job is to help our offspring develop a rock-solid relationship with their Creator, one that is completely separate from ours. So how do we do that?

First, get your heart right. If you have doubts and questions, find a minister or clergy member to help you answer them. Your young children are not the right people with whom to share your concerns. Your job is to teach and guide them, not the other way around. And since kids see through hypocrisy faster than you can blink, make sure you believe what you teach.

Retired nurse and Christian counselor Joyce Stevens says, "Growing up, church was always important to me, and most of my friends were kids from church, but I did not know Christ until I was in my late forties. Even though we took our children to church every Sunday, the one we attended danced a bit when it came to words like sin and repentance.

"Through many twists through God's maze, we started attending Willow Creek Church in Barrington, Illinois. About that time, our son Paul, the one I always thought we would have problems with, had an experience similar to the scriptural Paul; he was literally knocked from his horse and made to see. One evening he sat us down and said, 'Mom, Dad, I want to tell you something.' He told us of his faith and then said that we were 'going out of this world sideways.'

"My first instinct was to respond as an insulted mom, but the Lord said, 'Be quiet.' I was, and we thanked Paul for what he'd said.

"Several weeks later, while I was driving on the Kennedy expressway, the Lord said, 'Joyce, it's time.' I said yes. Only weeks later, my husband, Gene, was led to the Lord in a completely different way.

"This is my encouragement to parents: don't ever underestimate the Lord, for he has his own agenda. Worrying and fussing about children who are temporarily off track makes not a bit of difference; the Lord knows what he is doing.

"After we came to Christ, we shared what had happened with our son Andy, who said that unless he saw the wounds on Christ's hands, he could not believe. Today Andy, his wife, and their children are all born again.

"Sometimes kids need us to cut them a little slack. God is much more concerned for their salvation than we are; too much pushing can drive them away. It's a fine line we must walk. The great news is that our grandkids are now bringing their friends to Christ—and the generations go on. All I can say is, 'Yay, God!'"

Second, once you have your heart right with God, walk the walk. If you believe church attendance matters, then go as a family. Regularly discuss what everyone learned, and ask questions about what your children believe. Sometimes you'll be amazed at their insightful answers; other times you'll be completely shocked by how they've misunderstood or missed certain important truths. Unless you talk about these things, you'll never know what's in your children's hearts. They won't generally come out with deep spiritual questions unless you set the scene for a safe, nonjudgmental dialogue beforehand. Kids want answers. Gently, carefully, guide them to the truth.

Realize that when you first start asking your kids for specific things they learned during the sermon, they'll squawk and call it an inquisition. However, they will also pay closer attention if they know you'll be asking questions afterward. Push a bit if you have to. Don't let them get by with gloss-overs like, "We talked about Joseph." Follow up with, "Great. What did you learn about Joseph that you didn't already know?"

Third, be transparent. I don't mean airing all your personal questions; I mean telling your children what you've been learning. Let them see you fail and watch how you handle it. None of us are superspiritual and do everything right. When I get frazzled and bark at everyone in my family, I need to humble myself and apologize. When I say something about someone else that I shouldn't, my children need to see me make it right. That way they'll understand that I don't live a perfect life—though I try—and it will help them as they live out their own faith.

114

Especially as they go through the teen years, how much our children trust and confide in us is directly related to the consistency of our lives. If they catch even a whiff of phoniness, they won't view us as a trustworthy guide and confidant. Genuineness is hugely important, so we must live what we believe.[3]

Fourth, actively cultivate your relationship with God. You can't take your children further spiritually than where you are yourself. For example, Ephesians 4:26 tells us, "'In your anger do not sin': Do not let the sun go down while you are still angry." Since everyone gets angry, we must teach our children how to deal with their anger as well. However, if anger and holding grudges are serious issues for me, I can't teach my children how to handle these emotions until I admit I have a problem. The old do-as-I-say-not-as-I-do won't work. But if I'm working on an issue and asking God's help in conquering it, that's something different. Then I can enlist my children's help in keeping me accountable.

Pray Together

This seems basic, but I'm amazed at the number of families, even those who are regular churchgoers, who don't even pause before meals to thank God for the food. Get your children involved. Praying a standard prayer may be fine when they're very young and even on occasion when they're older, but start giving them chances to pray aloud.

Lead by example and then give the children a turn. When you get one-sentence prayers of "thanks for the food," encourage them to go a bit deeper each time. Like everything else, praying out loud gets easier with practice.

Personal Devotions

Do you set aside a regular time each day to read Scripture, meditate, and pray? If not, start now. This time is vital to your relationships with God and with those in your family. The Bible is God's love letter to us and his instruction manual on how to live. Through regular time alone with him, reading his Word, we find out how he wants us to live.

Parenting is the most important job we'll ever have. It just makes sense to ask for help from the one who not only designed families, but who made each of our children.

Let your children see you have devotions. Tell them you're going into your room for your quiet time and they need to leave you alone. At first, they won't like not having your undivided attention, but if you stand firm and let them know this is really important, they will learn to respect that.

There are some great kids' devotional books available. As soon as your children can read on their own, purchase devotionals for them, and encourage them to spend a few minutes each day alone with God. Also, teach them early to open their Bibles to the recommended passages, not just to read the little story that goes along with it. The Bible is the most important part of the equation.

Family Devotions

These are so hard to do, but so important. Try very hard. Don't let crazy schedules derail your plans. Speaker Gaye Martin says, "We tried desperately to have family devotions, which is harder to do than getting into a girdle wet. We tried many forms of devotions, and when the children got into their teens, we finally settled on afternoons. We would evenly divide up a chapter in the Bible, and whichever people were available would read several verses. Then I'd ask them to tell me their favorite verse—my attempt to get them to at least scan the verses they didn't read.

"One day Scott and Steve were home, and since Scott was getting ready for a date, he was in a hurry. Steve, with halo firmly fixed over his horns, asked, 'Aren't we going to do devotions first?' Of course I said yes. Scott sighed, and they randomly picked Psalm 132. With only seventeen verses, I felt it was a safe and quick devotion. As each read their fair share, the other would taunt and tease about pronunciation and how long this was taking. Meanwhile, I was asking God if he could possibly be in the midst of such chaos. I told him this was wasted time as far as I could see. How in the world could he break into such frustration?

"When I finished with the devotion, Steve said, 'Couldn't we read another?'

"I knew this was a direct hit on Scott, but as I started to refuse, I noticed that Psalm 133 was only three verses. So I told Scott, 'Let's do this one, and then you are out of here.'

"Psalm 133 reads, 'Behold, how good and how pleasant it is for brethren to dwell together in unity!' (KJV). Both boys are now men in their forties who can quote this psalm verbatim. I know that time was not wasted."

Sometimes we've done better at this than at other times. Often we've encouraged personal devotions and neglected family ones. Both are so important. Find a booklet or guide, and spend a few minutes after a meal in family worship. Don't give up, even in the midst of chaos.

Church Involvement Matters

Rick Warren, in his book *The Purpose-Driven Life*, says there are two kinds of church people: attenders, who are really spectators in the life of a church, and members, who are committed and involved. Which kind are you?

As your children get older, and certainly by the time they hit their teens, they need to learn that church is not just a place for them to go to see their friends and be entertained. God wants more from them than to simply show up in his house on a semiregular basis. The unique talents and abilities he has gifted us with are to be used in his kingdom. As your children are exploring and discovering their special gifts and talents, encourage them to find ways to use them in your local church.

When we're on the fringes, outsiders looking in, it is easy to find fault. I've often said, "Those who do not help may not complain." I say it to our teens, since the number-one gripe of teens everywhere is, "This is BORING." Nine times out of ten, it springs from being a spectator, not an active participant.

Look for ways to get your children plugged into your church's ministry, whether it's helping in the nursery, children's church, the kitchen, grounds clean-up, or whatever. Your children have something to give and contribute. By your example and encouragement, they will go from being bored to being actively involved.

I had a youth pastor who spent years quoting a paraphrase of Luke 12:48: "To whom much is given, much will be required." After a while, all he'd say was, "To whom," and I'd know what he meant, though it bugged me to no end at the time. He wanted me to understand that it was my job to use the gifts God had given me for his glory. We must raise the standard and teach our children the same thing. If we expect nothing from them, we'll get nothing.

Church as Worship, Not Drudgery

What attitude do you carry into church with you? Does everyone in your household—including you—moan and groan about going? If so, what does that say to your children?

Church is not really about us. The worship services are our opportunity to join with other Christians in offering our hearts in worship to God. If we go to see what God is going to do for us, we're going for the wrong reasons. A word from the Holy Spirit may be an unexpected blessing, but our motivation for going should be to give God praise. This is often hard to teach children, whose main focus seems to be, "What's in it for me?" If we are asking the same question, we have a problem.

Get excited about opportunities to worship God. We live in a free country where we can gather without fear. That is a privilege many, many Christians around the world would give anything to have. Teach your children to value that privilege. Broaden your family's horizon by doing a bit of research on other countries. Find pictures and statistics and stories of real Christians, and start praying for them. The book *Operation World*, by Patrick Johnstone and Jason Mandryk, is a great prayer resource.

Lead by example, and get excited about worship. Bring positive emotions with you to church. Be an active participant, not just someone going through the motions. Attitudes—good and bad—spread faster than wildfires.

Know what you believe. Live it, and then seek to actively instill it in your children. It's the most important thing you'll ever teach them.

As you think about your children's spiritual training, ask yourself:

- What's my relationship with God right now?
- If I'm not happy with where I am spiritually, what am I going to do about it?
- Do my children know what I believe and what our church believes?
- How's my church attendance? Regular? Sporadic?
- Do I simply take my kids to church, or do we go together?
- Do we talk together about what we've learned?
- Have my children seen me having private devotions?
- Do I encourage my children to do the same?
- Do we take turns praying over meals?
- Do we have a family devotion time, even if it's not every day?
- What attitudes do I communicate about my church?
- Do I view church as opportunity or drudgery?
- Am I using my gifts and talents in our local church?
- Am I encouraging my children to do the same?

If you have late elementary/middle school children:

- Have I asked my children, point-blank, what their relationship is with God?
- Can they articulate their belief system?

- When was the last time my children heard me apologize when I've blown it?

If you have older teens:

- Are my teens involved in a ministry at our church?
- How do I answer cries of "It's boring"?
- Do I provide materials for my teens to have private devotions?
- Do I enlist my teens to help keep me accountable in my trouble areas?

8

Guys, Girls, and Hormones

When our daughter was in third grade, one of the class mothers asked Michele for her phone number. Thinking the woman meant to call me, Michele gave it to her. Next thing we knew, the lady's son started calling our house, asking for Michele. Seems he had a crush on her and asked his mother to get him Michele's number. Now, this child didn't simply call once. He called four and five times every day! We're talking third grade. After several days, my husband answered the phone and told the boy in no uncertain terms to stop calling our house.

I chaperoned more field trips than bear mentioning, so I know this scenario wasn't all that unusual. I was appalled at the number of parents who were actively encouraging boy-girl relationships in second and third grade and calling them "cute." That's crazy.

Growing Up Too Soon

There is a huge push in our society for children to grow up too fast. Crushes and dating will come soon enough. Don't push that on your young children, or on your teens either. Once they start traveling a certain road, they can't ever really back up, so don't send them in a direction they're not ready to go. Slow things down when you can. Never let TV and the great rallying cry of children everywhere—"But everybody's doing it"—deter you from what's right.

Fashion vs. Modesty

Take a stand. Elementary school children shouldn't dress like teens, and teens shouldn't dress like adults. Just because they fit into the size doesn't necessarily mean the garment is appropriate.

Several years ago, almost everywhere we looked in the mall, young girls' clothing had little cherries on it, along with slogans like, "You can't have my cherry," or "Stay away from my cherry." The girls—and quite a few parents—thought these were simply cute shirts and didn't realize that (even since I was a teen) "cherry" means virginity.

The clothing manufacturers aren't looking out for your kids. They're trying to make money, and they know sex sells in our society. Especially as your children get older, be prepared to do battle royal over appropriate clothing. Every concerned parent does. And since teens instinctively hate everything their parents like or stand for, you'll engage in everything from minor skirmishes to all-out warfare over this matter of clothing. My daughter and

I recently went school shopping, and I was appalled at what's being sold to young girls. Every year the clothes get shorter, tighter, and more revealing. Stand firm and don't cave in to the "But that's what everyone wears" argument.

As Christians, our clothing should reflect what we believe. Suggestive clothing is not appropriate, regardless of fashion. Do a careful check of your own closet too. Does your clothing send the wrong message? Teach your daughters and sons about modesty, which includes prohibiting bras and boxer shorts as outerwear.

Happening Hormones

As your kids hit puberty, hormones kick in, and things get wild and crazy. We're blessed to have two teens right now, and sometimes it's a wild ride. Remember that God wired guys and girls differently.

Guys are turned on primarily by sight. Teach your daughter to be careful that she's not causing a problem by what she wears. I often tell my daughter not to advertise something she's not selling. What I mean is that if she dresses trashy, guys will assume she's an easy mark. The way a woman dresses says a lot about how she sees herself. And if she dresses in revealing clothing, guys will see her as an object to be used.

Girls are primarily turned on by touch, though sight does play a part. Keep in mind that at the very time when your daughter is shying away from physical touch from parents, that's when she needs it most. Even if you feel awkward for a while (after all, her shape isn't the same as it was), keep those hugs coming, especially from dad.

A girl hungry for physical affection and touch is an easy target for a guy out for all he can get.

Defining Guy-Girl Relationships

Come late elementary school and middle school, you start hearing about kids "going out." This means they're an item, even though they don't actually GO anywhere. At least, most of them don't. There are always exceptions. Generally, kids who are "going out" walk to classes together and talk on the phone, but some go much further into serious kissing, fondling, and beyond. Keep a sharp eye on your kids' friends; know who calls the house and emails them on a regular basis. When they do have a first crush, be careful of stomping on their feelings. You don't want to make light of these new emotions, but you don't want to encourage them too much either. It's a fine line.

Teach your children early about setting the standards for physical contact. If they jump into too much physical familiarity, it's very hard to back up. With the next boy- or girlfriend, that line may get pushed back even further.

Not long ago I heard about a new practice among middle schoolers called "friends with benefits." Have you heard of this? I was dumbfounded. It means a guy and girl decide they're not officially going out; they're just friends, so they're free to go out with and flirt with anyone else they'd like. BUT they hold hands with and kiss their benefits friend. That's what "friends with benefits" means. You get all the "perks" of dating without any of the icky things like commitment or faithfulness.

I was even more appalled to learn that there are high schoolers who have taken this idea even further. They use "friends with benefits" to mean having sex with each other to gain experience and improve their sexual prowess.

Parents, be aware of what's going on with your teenagers, and err on the side of caution. Since dating and familiarity with the opposite sex is generally progressive, be careful. Focus on encouraging good, solid friendships with people of the same sex and large group activities involving both guys and girls, rather than one-on-one dating.

Rites of Passage

It used to be that there was a progression of privileges, rites of passage if you will, that began in middle school and went on into high school. For girls, first you shaved your legs, and then you wore pantyhose, started wearing lipstick, then nail polish, eye shadow, and so on. I'm guessing there were similar progressions for guys too.

Today I look around and see twelve-year-old girls wearing full makeup and fourteen-year-old guys with tattoos and nose rings. If they've done and seen it all before they hit middle or high school, where do they go from there? I believe the race through this progression is one of the reasons we're now seeing piercings and tattoos on younger and younger children. They want more, new, different. Today's "more" can lead to some questionable and scary things.

Parents, be careful that you keep your kids on a reasonable course when it comes to these things. Talk with other parents you know and respect about what they're doing and where they're setting the standards with their children. Don't cave in to everyone's-doing-it pressure. Whenever I tried that with my mom, I got an answer like, "If everyone jumped off a bridge, would you do it too?"

Jaca Mills remembers how her husband, Billy, solved this problem at their house. "When our daughter Marie was in middle and high school, whenever she wanted to do something we didn't want her to do, she'd try to use the same line all kids use: 'But everybody's doing it.'

"Whenever she'd say that, my husband would come back with, 'Name two.'

"At first she couldn't come up with one name, let alone two. But after a while, she'd always name the same two kids, so Billy came up with another response. After she gave those two names, Billy would say, 'Now name two that aren't doing it.'

"There were always at least two on that list too. But she got the point. Today, we still laugh about 'Name two.'"

Be prepared to counter your kids' arguments with ones from your side. And when all else fails, tell them that's the way it is, regardless of what others are doing. Period.

Permanent, or Passing Fad?

To me, the tattoo craze is a scary trend. Unlike wild-colored hair, tattoos can't be undone, at least not easily. Since more and more companies are banning tattoos, what your child begs for at sixteen he may regret by seventeen—and for the rest of his life. Another reason for saying no to tattoos is increasing information that tattoos may be linked to a rise in certain types of hepatitis. Experimenting with their looks is part of the identity struggle of the teen years, but be very, very careful about allowing anything that could risk your teens' health or have permanent consequences.

Swinging Moods

Make sure your children understand that out-of-control moods and feelings are a normal, natural result of everything happening inside their bodies. They are not going crazy. They may be driving you nuts, but they're perfectly normal—for kids with hormones.

Some kids get weepy, others get angry, and sometimes they're both within thirty minutes. Hang in there, and remind them to do the same. It does get better.

A dad I know came home from work one day and reminded his daughter to hang up her wet towel—something he'd said several hundred times before. Next thing the poor man knew, his daughter burst into tears, shouted about how everyone was always down on her, flounced into her room, and threw herself on her bed, sobbing her heart out. This poor dad walked into the kitchen, leaned over to his wife, and whispered, "Hormones, right?"

His wife patted his back and whispered, "Right."

He visibly relaxed. "OK. Just checking."

The Dating Age

The "right" age for dating depends on the child. Sixteen seems to be a good average, but for some teens, that's still too young. You know your children. If they show no interest in dating, don't push. If they show too much interest in dating, pull the reins in a bit tighter. Better to hold them off for a while than to push too young. Ask yourself whether your teen is emotionally ready for a relationship. Is he mature enough to handle sexual pressure? Can your teen set limits for physical touching, respect curfews, and make wise decisions? Can he or she deal with a broken heart? These factors all enter into deciding the "right" age.

Your teens also need to understand that guys and girls want different things from relationships. Connie Grigsby and Kent Julian explain the differences this way. "Girls want relationship. They long for intimacy and connectedness. Teenage guys, on the other hand, have more physical impulses. They crave visual and sensual stimulation."[1]

Contrary to popular thinking that says it's only the girl's job to say no, teach your teens that purity is each person's responsibility, for themselves as individuals and for their relationship. Grigsby and Julian, as well as other parenting experts, concur. They remind us that guys should practice self-control and show respect for girls by not allowing their hands to wander into forbidden zones. Girls should dress modestly so as not to make the guy's job harder and be prepared to call a halt or time-out if things are in danger of getting out of hand.

Sadly, our magazines and newspapers abound with stories of girls who found out the hard way that giving in to a guy never gains them the love and closeness they're looking for. All too often, what they really get is a broken heart or, worse, an unwanted pregnancy or sexually transmitted disease and the death of their dreams for the future. Make sure your daughter understands that—in her head *and* in her heart. Use statistics and/or real-life examples, but do whatever it takes to bring this truth home.

Also explain to your teens that crushes and attraction are normal, but they shouldn't get sucked into a relationship just because someone asks them to or because everyone's doing it and they don't want to feel left out.

Teach your girls how to say no graciously, and teach your boys how to ask politely and handle rejection. It will happen, but they'll get through it.

Teen Depression

Teen suicide and depression are growing tragedies in our country. Many times we don't ever know exactly what went wrong, though a breakup with a boyfriend or girlfriend is often named a contributing factor. Teens don't see beyond tomorrow. If life seems awful and unbearable today, they're sure it will never, ever get any better.

Talk openly with your kids. Tell them that rejection happens, but it's not the end of the world. Let them know they can talk to you—about anything. Also, make it your business to know the warning signs: if your teen is suddenly withdrawn, has no interest in anything, starts giving all her possessions away, and talks about dying, get help. Don't wait. It's too important.

Remind your kids that sometimes feelings get in the way of the facts and can't always be trusted. I've told them, "If Harry and I have a fight about something, I could feel like he doesn't love me, but that wouldn't make it true. I might be hurt and angry, but his love for me doesn't change because we had a fight." Feelings can be wrong. Help them learn to distinguish between emotions and facts, and remind them to hang in there, because feelings aren't always reliable.

Help your kids put life into perspective. What seems horrible today will not seem quite so bad tomorrow. High school is not the end of their life; it's merely a stepping-stone on the road, the beginning of the rest of the journey.

How to Treat a Lady

How husbands treat wives will have a huge impact on how sons treat their girlfriends and future wives. And how daughters allow men to treat them will also be a result of what they see their parents do. Teach sons to be polite and open doors for ladies. Teach them to offer grandma an arm to cross the street.

Harry and I have been married for nine years, but he still refers to me as his bride. Just hearing that makes me feel special and cherished, though I feel far from bride-like most days. But he holds me in high esteem, and that makes me want to be worthy of the title.

One of the "eight rules for dating my daughter" that has circulated on the Internet reminds prospective dates that if they pull up in the driveway and toot the horn, they'd better be delivering a package—because they sure aren't picking anyone up. Dads, don't hesitate to let a young man know that you value your daughter far more than he does his car, so she'd better get new-car treatment. Be clear on curfews and expectations, and make sure there are stiff consequences for blowing them off. Then follow through.

The Talk: When and How

Kids talk about sex all the time, and peer pressure to give in goes on all the time too. Today, oral sex is a huge problem—even in middle schools—because kids have convinced themselves that as long as it isn't intercourse, it isn't really sex. Sit your kids down and define exactly what you mean by purity and what the term "sex" encompasses. Make sure your sons and daughters understand that God invented sex and thinks it's a great idea FOR MARRIED PEOPLE. The problem is that sex drives don't magically kick in during the wedding ceremony. Things would certainly be easier if God flipped a switch after the "I do" and *whoosh*, instant sex drive.

This idea that teens are going to have sex anyway so we'd better supply them with plenty of condoms is insulting to our teens. It implies that young people are animals who respond solely on instinct and have no control over their bodies or actions. Baloney. It's a question of self-discipline.

Nobody said it was easy, but abstinence is possible. Prior planning is the key. The backseat of a car is way too late to set standards for sexual behavior. Start talking long before your children start dating. Discuss potentially dangerous situations to avoid, and make sure your teens know that if they land in trouble, they can call you to come get them out.

I've told my children about the time I let a young man walk me too far into the woods. We exchanged a few kisses, and when he pushed for more, I tried to ease away, but he wouldn't let me go. Actually, he said I wasn't leaving until he said I could. I was terrified. Fortunately, he did finally release me, but I learned a valuable lesson: groups are safer.

Don't let anyone convince your daughter that if a guy buys her dinner or takes her out, she "owes" him anything, sexual or otherwise. No way. And even if "everyone" is doing it, she doesn't have to.

When I was in eighth grade, my teacher and the other students ridiculed me for being a virgin. Whether the others lied to look cool, I don't know, but it was hard to be the only one. Support your kids. Applaud them when they stand up for what's right.

During high school, a good friend of mine began dating an older guy. She and her mom are both Christians, so I was shocked when her mom bought her birth control pills. My friend wasn't sure she was ready to have sex, but her mom told her the guy wouldn't wait forever, so she'd better give in if she didn't want to lose him. That's terrible advice. When my daughter was twelve, her father gave her a beautiful promise ring that she wears as a reminder of her commitment to purity.

Set the standard high, and teach your kids self-discipline and self-control. They can say no. And then they'll have the added benefit of a wedding night without the possibility of disease or a past to overcome.

Selective Telling

Sometimes too much information is not a good thing. There are certain details of your past that should stay in your past. If you say, "I did this, but . . ." chances are your children will tune out before you get to the regrets. They'll only hear the part about your doing such-and-such.

Don't give too much information, and think things through in advance so you're not caught off guard. Don't be afraid to say, "There are certain things I don't want to discuss with you right now, and that's one of them." Always give your kids an answer, but don't give any more details than you feel are appropriate.

Know your kids, and always, always stress purity. Poor choices in this area can create lifelong scars, so smart choices and clear plans are always the best defense.

Privacy, Pornography, and the Internet

If you have access to the Internet, make sure you know what your kids are doing online. We have told our kids that we must have a copy of their passwords. We're not going to read their email without a good reason, but if we suspect a problem, we won't hesitate to find out what's going on. The same goes with their rooms. Kids are fiercely protective of their privacy, but don't hesitate to violate it if you think there's good reason to do so.

Pornography is a huge concern today, especially online. It's incredibly easy to get and such a huge temptation, especially for guys. Explain frankly why pornography is wrong: it is degrading to women, shows them as objects, and turns something God intended to be a private and beautiful act between two married people into something cheap and trashy.

Also, when it comes to this issue, make sure your kids know how to respond if they run across it at someone else's home. I visited the home of friends of a friend one day. The couple had a four-year-old son and lived in a lovely, beautifully decorated home. Imagine my surprise when I went into the hall bath, and there, in a lovely wicker basket beside the toilet, was a stack of *Playboy* magazines. Teach your children to be like Joseph and run from sexual temptation.

Your Child's Future Spouse

There is much more about this topic we could cover, but think about one more question: have you thought about whom your child will marry someday? That person is already walking this earth. Start praying for this as-yet-unknown person. Pray that he or she will stay pure and follow Christ. Pray that your child's future mate will make good choices and grow close to God so that someday your son or daughter will get a fabulous spouse.

As you prepare your children to deal with guys, girls, and hormones, ask yourself:

- Do my children know our family standards for appropriate dress?
- Am I modeling those standards?
- How do they see me talk to and treat my spouse?
- Have I taken a firm stand against pornography?
- Have my spouse and I decided how we'll handle questions about dating and sex?
- Have we thought through our own pasts and decided how much or how little information to share with our children?

If you have late elementary/middle school children:

- Do my children know what to expect from puberty?
- Am I pushing them into dating too soon?
- Have I started early in telling my children about the rules for future dating?
- Have I talked with them about God's design for sex?
- Have I encouraged them to take a strong stand for abstinence and purity?
- How am I helping them keep that commitment?

If you have older teens:

- When was the last time I hugged my teen?
- Do I know my teen's friends?
- Do my sons know how to treat a lady?
- Do my daughters know what kind of behavior to expect from a date?
- Have I talked frankly about the progressive nature of familiarity with the opposite sex?
- Have I given my teens strategies for dealing with peer pressure about sex?
- Do my children know what to do if they ever get themselves into a bad situation?
- Am I praying for their future spouses?

9

Exercise and Health

Nearly half of American youths aged 12–21 years are not vigorously active on a regular basis," reports the Centers for Disease Control.[1] Along with the decrease in physical activity has come an alarming increase in childhood obesity and diabetes.

However, there is good news for parents. Emerging data is showing that for active children, the benefits are not only physical, but mental as well. More and more researchers are studying the connection between physical fitness and improved scores on standardized tests and are confirming what doctors—and parents—have long known: active kids are able to think more clearly.

If we want our children to reap all the benefits of physical fitness, there is really only one way to do it: leading by example. Go for a walk together instead of watching TV. Ride a bike, go for a swim, skate, or play catch.

The habits your children form in childhood will follow them throughout their lives. Remember when your mother told you to go play outside? Mine used to lock the door behind me so I couldn't tromp back inside whining that I didn't have anything to do. Install a basketball hoop; keep footballs, softballs, baseball gloves, Frisbees, and other sports equipment around.

As our kids have gotten older, movies and video games have become more of a problem. Friends come over, and before you turn around, they've been huddled in front of the screen for four hours. Nope. We tell ours that is not an option. They need to go outside and find something else to do. And if they say there isn't anything, well, I have my infamous list of yucky chores.

Stress Reduction

Even kids get stressed in our fast-paced world, and exercise is one of the best stress relievers. It's especially critical during puberty, so make physical activity part of your kids' lives from the beginning. Encourage them to try a sport, whether it's in a casual recreational league or a more competitive school or city league. Especially after they've been cooped up at school all day, they need that exercise time. Make sure they get it.

But I'm Fat

About the time kids hit middle school, everyone's weight becomes a major topic of conversation among both boys and girls. Kids with a larger frame are made fun of, and kids who are overweight are laughed at, almost as much as those who are too skinny or too short.

We know a young man who doesn't "do outside." Except to walk to and from the bus stop, he sits in his house and watches TV or plays video games. Sadly, he's overweight, and that won't get better unless he makes some changes.

Be tough with your kids on this issue. Whether their exercise is structured or not, make sure they spend regular time outside doing something active.

Talk with your children about eating disorders. Tell them that the scale is not the only measure of how healthy they are. Muscle weighs more than fat, so if you've raised athletes, they're going to weigh more. That's not only OK, that's good. But since eating disorders are a serious problem in teens, especially girls, know the warning signs, and don't be afraid to intervene if your child seems headed in that direction.

Help your children develop a healthy body image. What they see in magazines is NOT a healthy image. Also, make sure your children understand that calories are not the only indicator of what they should eat. I've seen overweight girls turn up their noses at meat and refuse to eat regular meals, yet they continuously snack on chips and soda, saying there aren't too many calories in those. There is clearly a gap in their nutritional education.

Food as Fuel

Our kids need to understand that food is intended as fuel for their bodies. If they want top performance from their "engine," they need to be fueling it with healthy stuff. The closer something is to its natural state, the better it is for them. Fresh fruit beats potato chips every time. The calories may be the same, but the nutritional value is completely different. One is good for them; the other is mostly empty calories.

As in most parenting issues, modeling is key. Keep healthy snacks like fruits and veggies, peanut butter, and salads around the house. Limit the amount of junk food you keep in the pantry, and offer healthier alternatives.

Start your kids eating veggies and fruit early so this won't become an issue later. Read nutritional labels, and try to limit the amount of sugar in your family's diet. I've been checking lately and am amazed at how much sugar there is in foods like tomato sauce, of all things.

Also, try to stay away from the partially hydrogenated fats. Those are the ones that form "bad" cholesterol, because your body can't digest them. Manufacturers use them because they extend a food's shelf life. Try to avoid them in your family's diet whenever possible.

If your teen talks about dieting and that's a realistic concern, check with your doctor first, and then help your child choose healthy foods. Even if they're stubborn teens, don't throw up your hands and say you can't tell them what to eat anymore. Sure you can. Eliminate junk food as a snack option, and pretty soon fruit and nuts are going to look really good.

The USRDA What?

Make sure your children understand basic nutrition, what the USRDA means, and how to read food labels. Not all foods are created equal, so your children need to learn how to tell the difference between empty calories and power foods and how to eat a balanced diet. Also, explain portion size. The first time I took out a measuring cup and poured in what the cereal label calls a serving, I laughed out loud. You might want to try that with your kids. It's a real eye-opener.

Doctor, Doctor

When your kids get sick, chances are you nag them to take the medicines the doctor prescribes. Someday you won't be there to do that. Teach children to take responsibility for their health and body. Ultimately, they will be the best judges of what is normal for them. Don't let them get into the habit of popping a pill for every ache, and make sure they understand the danger of masking symptoms. Make sure your children know when they should see a doctor and how to find a good one. Also, be sure your daughters learn how to do regular breast self-exams.

Dream Time

Statistics tell us that because of how quickly they're growing and changing, very young children and teenagers need huge quantities of sleep. Yet most teens get less than ever.

Smart parents set bedtimes, which benefit everyone in the family. Children need sleep, and parents need time to reconnect as a couple and take a breather from parenting responsibilities. Be prepared for battle, though, because children hate bedtimes. They're afraid they'll miss out and are convinced all sorts of fun stuff happens the minute they hop into bed. They're also quite comfy at the center of your world.

For early elementary kids, 7:30 to 8:00 p.m. is a good bedtime. I was always amazed when parents told me their kids stayed up until 11 p.m. or later—on school nights. Set a bedtime and stick to it. Stand firm in enforcing consequences.

Actually, going to bed and getting up at the same time every day is best for our bodies. Try to model that for your children. Even as children mature and bedtime gets later, guard your time with your spouse at the end of the day. One solution is to institute an in-room time, with lights-out slightly later.

Since some children need more sleep than others, watch your children for a while, and see how long they sleep if no alarm wakes them. (I don't mean your teen who stayed up until 3:00 a.m. playing video games and is now sleeping the day away.) Children who can't get up and moving in the mornings need more sleep. You may have to play hardball to make sure they get it. Do it. It's important.

Drugs and Alcohol

Though today's school systems seem to be doing a fairly decent job of covering these issues, the responsibility for making sure kids learn and understand the dangers rests with parents. Communicate, communicate, communicate.

Good friends of ours Kyle and Tammy Johnson have talked long and loud with their kids about this issue. Now they've turned it into a family saying: "Clean your room. Don't do drugs." The kids laugh, but they know Mom and Dad are serious. These parents have clearly stated that drug and alcohol use are strictly in the no-way-no-how category and that disobedience will reap swift and serious parental discipline. Spell it out.

I asked my kids about the first time they'd been offered marijuana and how they responded. One said sixth grade, the other seventh, and both had responded, "No way." I was proud of their response but frightened at how soon they had to deal with this. Don't be an ostrich. The offer will be made, if it hasn't been already. Make sure your kids are ready to deal with it.

Experts tell us that children's personalities and what's happening in their lives impact their susceptibility to alcohol or drug use. If your children are dealing with a major stressor—a move, new school, major breakup, divorce or death in the family—be especially attuned to what's going on, since this is when your teens are most vulnerable. Research and public-service campaigns remind us of an important truth: parents are what keep kids off drugs. Don't wait for the "right moment." Talk with your kids. Often. And when you think you've said it enough, say it again.

As you think about raising healthy kids, ask yourself:

- Am I preparing healthy meals for my family?
- Do we all drink water regularly, or is soda the beverage of choice?
- How much sugar do we consume every day?
- Are we eating the recommended daily allowance in every category?
- What's in my pantry? Mostly junk?

- Is my fridge stocked with healthy foods?
- Do I exercise regularly? If not, how can I start immediately?
- Do I get enough sleep?
- Do we all take a multivitamin daily?
- What do we need to change or improve?

If you have late elementary/middle school children:

- When was the last time I talked with my children about drugs and alcohol?
- Do they know my position on these important issues?
- Have we talked through a plan if they find themselves pressured in these areas?
- What do my kids do after school?
- Do they spend time outside doing something physical every day? If not, how can I get them into this habit?
- What activities could our family try to become more active?
- Do my kids get enough sleep?
- Do they have a regular bedtime?

If you have older teens:

- Do my teens have a healthy body image?
- Can they read food labels?
- Have we discussed ways to deal with extra stress in their lives?

- Have I been honest about eating disorders and their dangers?
- Do I make sure our teens get enough sleep?
- Do my daughters know how to do a breast self-exam?
- Do my teens know when they need a doctor and how to choose one?
- Do they understand medicine's purpose and the dangers of overmedicating and masking symptoms?

10

Melding Home Life
with Friend Life

During a long-distance car ride when Diane Burke's sons were young, the boys got restless. They argued constantly, poked at one another, and were making each other miserable. In an attempt to get them to focus on something besides their disagreements, she proposed they play a verbal game. She asked, "If you could be any animal in the world, what animal would you be?"

Her oldest son answered, "I would be a horse 'cause they're beautiful and can run like the wind."

Without hesitation, her second son answered, "I would be an elephant 'cause they're big and strong and can step on horses."

Can't you picture those two rascals in the backseat? Don't they sound just like your children? Today the Burkes laugh about that story and the car trip that inspired it. Over the years it has become part of their family's oral history, something to be remembered and retold at family events.

Every family is unique, with its own traditions, practices, and celebrations that bind members together and get passed from one generation to the next. When children are very young, the family unit is their whole world and the cornerstone around which their identity is formed. Later on, friends and outside influences are added, and children must reevaluate where they fit in life. The push-pull relationship between friends and family increases with the teen years as children test their wings. How do we help our children gradually prepare for life outside our nest without shoving them out into the world too soon? The balance between holding too tight and abdicating leadership isn't always easy to find, but hopefully this chapter will provide some help.

Family Mealtimes

I've seen countless homes where the kitchen table has been turned into a home office or craft area. When I ask how anybody eats there, parents say, "Oh, we all just eat in front of the TV, or everyone does their own thing." These parents are missing out on one of the best opportunities to connect with their children and influence them for good. More than one study has shown that children whose families eat together on a regular basis—and communicate while they're together—are less likely to drink, smoke, use illegal drugs, have sex at young ages, get into fights, and get suspended from school, and they have a lower risk of suicidal thoughts.[1]

The practice of talking together and sharing your day helps children feel connected and prevents loneliness and isolation. Kids who feel alone at home will seek confirmation and affirmation elsewhere. Kids develop their view of themselves based on how the members of their family see them, so make your home a safe haven. If you solicit your children's opinions and give them time to share both frustrations and victories, you confirm their worth and value as members of the family. And mealtime is also a great time to learn what's going on in your children's lives and stay on top of who their friends are.

If your schedule is like ours, getting everyone rounded up is a lot like herding cats. Get two corralled over here, and one wanders off. Get that one back, and another has escaped. It isn't easy, but it is worth every moment of the effort.

Sometimes this means we don't eat until later in the evening. That's OK. Making the time is a worthwhile investment. My husband gets up incredibly early in the morning so he can be home for dinner. If he has to work late and I give our children the option of eating at the regular time or waiting until he gets home, they almost always choose to wait. The time matters to them too.

During the meal we don't answer the phone, because this is our time, our chance to reconnect and find out about everyone's day. It's also our chance to laugh together, because laughter makes it easier to deal with the hard things that come our way.

If family meals aren't a priority at your house, make the change now. Schedule time on the calendar—even if it's just once a week—and stick to it.

Family Meetings

Some families schedule meetings regularly to check on what's happening in everyone's lives. Other families hold them sporadically or on an as-needed basis. We brainstorm vacation plans and dreams once a year, but we've also met at other times to discuss important issues or decisions. These meetings can also be used to set up family policies or deal with sticky topics. Make sure, though, that these don't become a downer for your kids. Always end on a positive note, and balance correction with love and encouragement for things done well.

Birthdays

Make a big deal out of the day of your children's birth. You don't have to throw an expensive party, but make sure your children understand their importance to you and your family.

Set a special table. Cook their favorite meal. For younger kids, make a crown and declare them king or queen for the day. Let them know how much you love them and how glad you are that they belong to your family.

Tell stories about the day they were born and the cute things they did when they were young (even if that was only last year). Laugh together about how tiny they once were. Haul out photos and videos. Your teens will roll their eyes, but they love hearing the stories of their lives. This is part of instilling their heritage.

Tell stories about when you were young too, so they feel connected to the previous generation. When my brother and I were kids, Mom made birthdays an important day. We could always count on receiving a can of mandarin oranges and a can of pineapple chunks. Those were two of our favorite treats, but my folks couldn't afford them on a regular basis. On our birthday, however, we could sit down with a spoon and finish the cans all by ourselves—no sharing with anyone. It's a memory that still makes me smile.

When children are young, we help them remember to make or buy gifts and cards for their parents and family members, but by the time they're teens, the responsibility must slowly shift to their shoulders. This may require a creative approach. To help our teens grasp this, I started mentioning what I'd like for my birthday several weeks prior to the day. Even though it felt awkward and selfish, I'd throw out statements like, "In case anyone's wondering, I'd really like a new cosmetic bag for my birthday this year. And in case you forgot what day it is, I circled it on the calendar, in red." They laughed, but a few days later, a trip to the mall became desperately and mysteriously urgent.

While I truly appreciated the lovely cosmetic bag, the gift wasn't really the point. I wanted them to look beyond their own needs and invest time and money in someone else, just because. Try it with your family. And if you have a giftless birthday, gently tell them how it made you feel, and try again with the next family member's birthday. Hopefully they'll grasp the concept of giving to others and carry it with them into adulthood.

Holidays

Kids love the familiarity of traditions, and everyone has certain things that make holidays special and meaningful for them. Grab a piece of paper and jot down the special things your family does from year to year during the Christmas season. What about Thanksgiving? Easter? Take a minute to consider which activities bring great joy and which bring stress. Ask your family these same questions. Seeing both good and bad on paper may help you reevaluate what you're doing.

Traditions grow and change over time. Sometimes we make room for new traditions, and at other times, we change the approach. Baking Christmas cookies with the kids has always been part of our holiday routine. Interest has waned lately, though we still do it and have fun together. OK, the no-help-no-eat rule is probably the deciding factor, but we're still enjoying ourselves.

When I was a single parent, time was my most precious commodity. I finally ditched the guilt and bought premade cookie dough, which went against every tenet of good German moms. But I realized the dough wasn't the issue; the important part was the time we spent laughing and reminiscing about previous Christmases.

Friends of ours bake a gingerbread house every year. Others bake certain cookies or candy; another family goes to see the Nutcracker ballet. We cut down our own Christmas tree every year, which seems rather mundane, except that we live in central Florida, which is not known for its pine forests. Some years we show up at the tree farm in shorts; other years we sip hot chocolate and shiver. But we always laugh about the first year we did this and bought a tree so wide we could hardly get from one room to the next.

At Thanksgiving, we go around the table and list the things we're thankful for. Since the first year—when the food got cold before we got halfway around the table—we now do that after we eat. But it's important to verbally recount our many blessings.

Perhaps your family didn't make a big deal about holidays when you were growing up. Or maybe all you have are bad memories. Here's your chance to change things for your family. Ask some friends what they do, and experiment with a few things. Figure out what works for your gang.

Most traditions aren't big, elaborate, or costly. They're simply things you do from year to year. Harry's mom gave us a ceramic Christmas village that we look forward to setting up every December.

In everything, don't lose sight of the fact that people are far more important than fine china or elaborate celebrations. In November, we block out several December nights on the family calendar as "family time." During these little breaks in the holiday hustle and bustle, we stay home and hang out by the fire or play a game together. That too has become a tradition.

No family's holiday celebration actually looks anything like a Norman Rockwell painting or Hallmark commercial. That's fantasy. If you try to create that, you'll be frustrated, and so will your family. Don't lose the reason we celebrate to begin with. A lady I know was so determined to have the "perfect" holiday every year that she ran herself ragged. She baked until the wee hours, decorated everything just so, planned an elaborate meal, and served it on a beautifully set table. But by the time dinner was served, she was tired and cranky, everyone else was stressed too, and nobody had any fun.

Traditions also need to be flexible. Since we can't round up the entire extended family exactly on December 24, we regularly schedule "early Christmas" in mid-December for whoever can make it. One year it was warm enough to get out on the lake, so we took a vote. We could serve a fancy turkey dinner and half the people would stay home all day to prepare it, or we could put frozen, store-bought lasagna in the oven and all go boating. Plan B won hands down, and we still talk about the year we went boating in December.

Making Memories

Certain occasions are what my sister-in-law calls "memory makers"—an eightieth birthday party, weddings, graduations, special trips. When these special times come up, plan to take plenty of pictures, enjoy every moment, and then relive those times together over the years. That adds continuity to your children's lives. When the clan gets together, we spend hours playing "remember when."

The Great Photo Caper

I envy anyone whose family photos are carefully cropped and preserved in scrapbooks. I have piles of boxes stashed under a tablecloth beside the front door. Since I figure I'll be seventy-five before I find time to scrapbook, I've found a compromise I can live with. I bought photo albums that include little memo spaces to write in the important facts like names, dates, and places. You slip in the accompanying photos, and voilà, photo album. That way my children can enjoy the photos—and I'm free of the guilt of the boxes behind the front door.

Snow Drifts and School Papers

If you're not careful, the papers that cascade out of school backpacks can bury you alive. I found a method—and I use the term loosely—for keeping our papers under control. I (try to) regularly sort papers and save only the really important ones, usually ones that demonstrate our children's creativity in some way. At the end of the school year, those go in a large, zippered plastic bag and then get stashed in each child's "memory box." Someday they can go through the bags and pitch whatever they don't want, but for now, I'm corralling the important stuff. Take heart, the piles do get smaller as they get older.

What's in a Name?

Do you have nicknames for your children? Pet names for your spouse? When I was a child, my mom called me "Connie-mouse." I'm not sure how it started, but it stuck. While my friend's mothers yelled their full names if they were in trouble, I always knew things were bad when Mom dropped the "mouse" and just yelled "Connie!"

My husband and I call each other "Schatz," which means "treasure" in German. We also have pet names we call our children, but we're careful where we use them. We don't want to make something that's special at home become a reason for ridicule in public.

Most nicknames evolve naturally. Some are given on purpose. If your kids don't have pet names, think about starting some. These become part of their identity, their family connectedness. Just be careful that the nicknames are something they're comfortable with and not derogatory in any way.

Say That Again?

What about family sayings? Are there things you say over and over again? Little quips and quotes that are passed from generation to generation? Think about it. What phrase could your whole family repeat the moment you say the first word? These too are great ways to build continuity and togetherness in your family.

Conversely, though, beware of labeling your children, and watch what they overhear you saying to others. "This is my wild one. He's going to be a handful." Or, "We've got to watch her every minute." Remember that kids generally live up to parents' expectations. If you say one thing to them and something else about them, guess which one will have the most influence on their behavior?

Friends and Peer Pressure

Tempting though the idea is, we can't cover our children in bubble wrap to keep them from getting hurt or keep them forever in the house and solely under our influence. The older they get, the more important friends will be in their lives. However, that doesn't mean we should throw up our hands and assume we no longer have any influence over our children. As they reach toward adulthood, they need our input and support more than ever.

Parents, not peers, are the most influential people in the lives of teenagers. In fact, according to many researchers, the statistics of who has the most influence on teenagers flesh out like this: 1) Parents 2) Extended family 3) Adults outside the home—coaches, youth workers, teachers, and friends of parents 4) Peers and 5) Media—TV, movies and music. . . .

155

Peers have such an enormous influence on so many teens today because the top three influential groups—parents, extended family, and caring adults—are absent.[2]

That is a sobering reality and one to take seriously. Are we so busy, distracted, or wrapped up in our own lives that our teens are looking elsewhere for the support, companionship, and encouragement we should be giving? Reclaim the top step on your teen's "influence ladder," and also put some other adults in place whom your teen can go to for advice and help.

Of all the challenges children face, fitting in with friends is one of the toughest they deal with. The newspapers are filled with tragic stories of the extremes kids will go to for peer acceptance. Encourage your kids to see themselves as God sees them. Find out what their struggles are, and help them deal with those struggles. Your attitude will determine how far into their lives and hearts they will let you go. You want to be in a position to guide them, so make sure you've developed a caring, nurturing relationship and home life.

Conflict

There are times adolescence is oddly reminiscent of the terrible twos. No matter what parents say, it is met with resistance and complaints. Intellectually, parents know this is part of the process of our children thinking things through and learning to make their own decisions, but the constant questioning of our opinions and authority is wearying.

Remember that your attitude will define most situations. Don't allow your frustration to create an environment of constant nagging and criticism. Remind your older children that there are times (OK, many times) they won't agree with you, but they don't have to. Don't be afraid to say, "We hear your objection, and we respect your right to feel that way; however, this is not your decision to make. Your job is to live within the limits we set." This shows respect for them as people but keeps you firmly in the position of authority. It also lets children know you always love them—even when they disagree with you. Of course, if they ignore the rules, there will be consequences. Always keep the distinction clear between your love for them as people and your feelings about their actions or choices. Whenever possible, end such discussions on a positive note, not a negative one. Your children will learn to handle conflict by seeing how you handle it with them.

Every once in a while, when one of our children doesn't like something we've said, come dinnertime the child is suddenly not hungry. We say, "Fine. You don't have to eat anything, but you will sit at the table with us anyway, because that's what we do. If you choose not to eat, understand that the kitchen will be closed to you until breakfast in the morning." It usually doesn't take long before the conflict is forgotten and we're again enjoying our time together.

A Kid-Friendly Home

We encourage our children to invite friends over. This does two things: it ensures that we know where they are, and it gives us a chance to get to know their friends. We have tried to provide lots of things for them to do, like a basketball hoop, a volleyball net, and a trampoline.

We want our home to be a place kids like to hang out. I recently read about a mom who stocked the freezer with frozen pizza during her children's teen years. We're adopting that policy here. Since food and fun seem to go together, we want to provide both at our home.

Trust and Friends

A while back, one of our children chose a group of friends we didn't care for. These children had been sneaky more than once, treated our child shabbily, and always gave the impression they were laughing at us and testing how much they could get away with. Our child's requests to go out with this group were denied more than once. When our child complained, we said that privileges had to do not only with personal responsibility, but also with friend choices.

One mom named Kay says she learned this lesson when her oldest son was fifteen. "John had a friend named Mark, whose father was a state trooper. I felt Mark was a positive influence on our son, partly because of his father's position.

"One afternoon John came home after bike riding with Mark, bursting to tell me something. He finally blurted out that he and Mark had taken some cupcakes from the local grocery store without paying for them. I was shocked and immediately started to lecture John about stealing. 'You have to return the cupcakes.'

"He said, 'We can't, because we ate them.' I did not make him go to the store and confess, though maybe I should have. But I don't believe he ever did anything like that again.

"The lesson for me was that I shouldn't have relied on Mark's father being a police officer to exempt Mark from dishonest behavior. John is a fine, upstanding Christian today. I believe both he and I learned a lesson."

We've talked extensively with our children about how trust and privileges go together. When our children act responsibly and do what they should around the house, show respect for their parents, and choose good friends, they build up their trust account with us. The higher the balance in the trust account, the greater the freedom and privileges they have. However, bad friend choices, irresponsible behavior, and disrespect for us quickly draw down the trust account balance. When the trust account is low, so are the privileges. The two move together. Encourage your children to build up their trust accounts, and then award privileges accordingly.

Celebrate good choices and your children's incredible worth and value to your family. A loving, accepting home is one of the most lasting legacies we can give our children.

How are you doing in helping your children blend home and friends? Ask yourself:

- Do we regularly eat together as a family?
- Do I make a big deal out of my children's birthdays?
- Have I let them know how special they are?
- Do I tell them stories of when they were younger?
- Have I been telling them stories of my childhood?
- Do they know where their grandparents were born and what their lives were like?

- What are our family's holiday traditions?
- Have I explained to the children why we do certain things at holidays?
- If we don't have any traditions, which ones could we start? Ask for input from the kids.
- What are some of our family "memory makers"? Have we talked about them lately?
- Do I take photos or videos of the big and small events in my kids' lives? Have we looked at these pictures lately?
- Am I saving some of my kids' most important school papers?

If you have late elementary/middle school children:

- Do I know who their friends are?
- Am I careful to avoid using nicknames in front of their friends?
- Have I asked them which traditions are most important to them?

If you have older teens:

- Do I continue to make mealtimes, family nights, and holidays a priority? Do I expect my teens to be there?
- Do I solicit their opinions on world events?
- Have we discussed how trust and privileges work together?
- Am I helping my teens remember family members' birthdays and important events?

11

Manners and Speech

When my daughter was about four years old, she and I were in line at the grocery store one day when she spotted a man ahead of us with a rather large belly. Before I realized what was coming, she turned to me, wide-eyed, and stage-whispered, "Mommy, look at that man over there with a baby in his tummy." Shoppers three aisles over chuckled and studied the man in question, who was not amused. Had I not been blocked in by shopping carts, I would have made a quick getaway, but instead, I tried to explain that only ladies could have babies in their tummies. "But if there's no baby in there, why is his tummy so big?" she wanted to know. The shoppers laughed out loud, the man glared at me over his case of beer, and I wished the ground would swallow me up.

My daughter, though, was oblivious. Children do not understand etiquette, polite questions, or the right time and place to ask certain things. These things must be taught, just like "please" and "thank you." What may be amusing in a four-year-old is not funny in a teenager. Remember when "Yes, ma'am" and "No, sir" were the norm, not the exception? Many parents haven't been teaching—or enforcing—good manners and polite speech. Children will not learn these things by osmosis. They must be deliberately, consistently taught.

We spent the better part of a year getting rid of "Yeah" as the response to absolutely every question. Whenever we got yeahed, we'd ask, "Excuse me, what did you say?"

Pause. "Yes, Mom. Yes, Harry."

We'd grin. "Ah, that's what we thought you said."

Or we'd sit down to dinner, and someone would ask for the peas. "Was there a 'please' in there somewhere?"

Eye roll. Sigh. "Please pass the peas."

Another big grin from me. "Ah, that's what I thought you said."

Manners and polite speech are taught by repetition, pure and simple. There is no quicker, easier way. You have to harp on it until the right response becomes second nature. I've heard it takes twenty-one days to turn an action into a habit. I don't know if "please" and "thank you" will stick after twenty-one corrections or twenty-one days, but don't give up. Your children will eventually learn these things if you don't quit.

If you've ever sat across from someone at a meal who talked with his mouth full, you're familiar with another etiquette issue. Not very appetizing, yet we see it all the time. It's so easy to do. Someone says something, and you've got the perfect response. It's hard to wait until you finish chewing and swallow before you respond. But do. Be kind to your tablemates. And teach your children the same thing. I have to mentally catch myself before I fall back into the habit.

Addressing Adults

When we moved from south to central Florida, we realized we had moved far enough north to be in the South, since south Florida is mostly transplants from New York and New Jersey. Around here, there is still more respect shown to the older generation, but we see it eroding every day. Respect should not be optional. I introduce myself to children and teens as Miss Connie. My husband is known as Mr. Harry. Tell your children how to address their elders. Unless the adult tells them differently, require a title in front of an adult's name. Keep at it until your children show deference and respect without prompting.

Here's Your Change

Do your children know how to speak with store clerks and waiters or waitresses? Teach them to speak clearly and look the person in the eye. That too is a sign of respect. This is especially hard for teens, who tend to mumble on general principle and rarely look anyone in the eye. Still, it's important, so keep after them.

But, Teacher . . .

Sometimes your children will have to speak up to a teacher, coach, or other authority figure. Go over possible scenarios, and teach them when it is appropriate to disagree politely—and how to do it respectfully. A child who raises her hand and says, "I'm sorry, Mr. Smith, but I'm not sure I agree with you," will garner a completely different response than the child who bursts out, "You've got to be kidding. That's crazy."

Sometimes it's our job to go to bat for our children; other times they can handle it on their own. Obviously, the older they get, the more the responsibility will shift to their shoulders. By going to bat for them I don't mean shielding them from the consequences of their actions. Smart parents let children experience natural consequences. What I'm referring to is unfair situations or times when communication can solve a problem. My son recently emailed a teacher about his grade. He had some makeup work to do after an illness, which he did, but the grade does not reflect that. He's trying to get that resolved. If he were still in second grade, I'd call the teacher.

The Unruly Evil

In the Disney movie *Bambi*, Thumper's mother asks him if he remembers the rule. Head down and digging his toe in the dirt, the shamefaced little bunny says, "If you can't say something nice, don't say nothin' at all."

That's good advice. Teach your kids to hold their tongues. It's a good thing for adults to be reminded of as well, because our children are watching. I tell people I've started a new exercise program called biting my tongue. Some days it's tough, but I try to remember a sign I read recently that said, "Even a fish wouldn't get into trouble if he kept his mouth shut."

There is a good reason the book of James calls the tongue an "unruly evil." It gets everyone into trouble at one time or another. Haven't you said things and immediately wanted to call the words back? One of life's hard-but-critical lessons is that once words are said, they can never be unsaid.

We had to teach this at our house several years back. One of our children got angry and said some really ugly things to us. So we used an idea I'd read somewhere and told this child that every day after school X number of hours would be spent pounding nails into a board. Every afternoon for almost a week, that child worked up a sweat pounding nails and raised a few blisters in the process.

After a while, the nail box was empty, and the board was full of nails. We said, "Great work. Now take all the nails back out."

So our child spent several more days pulling the nails back out of the board. When the job was done, we asked, "Does the board look like it did before?"

"Nope. It's got holes in it."

"That's right," we said. "Those nails are like the words we say. When we say mean ones, they're like nails in someone's heart. We may apologize and take the nails out, but the scars in their hearts—like the marks in the wood—will always be there. They don't go away. An apology is the right thing to do and keeps the hurt from going on and on, but it doesn't undo the damage to hearts and relationships. Be very careful before you speak."

Teach your children the value of holding their tongues and not letting every word that pops into their heads cross their lips.

Psst, Guess What I Heard

I think the best thing about living in a small town is also the worst thing. The downside is that you have no real privacy—because everyone knows your business. But on the plus side, if you're in trouble, people will be right there—because everyone knows your business.

I've heard people throw out juicy tidbits—disguised as prayer requests—and then tack on, with nose slightly in the air, "There's much more to this sad situation, but I'm not at liberty to share it." They want you to know that they know more than you do. Ridiculous, isn't it? I heard a long time ago that if you're not part of the problem or the solution, you have no business in the discussion. Live it. Teach it. If you're caught in a situation where you inadvertently hear things you shouldn't, don't pass them on.

However, remind your children when it's OK to break a confidence. If they know something about, for example, a friend at school that indicates the friend could be in trouble somehow, telling you is not gossip. It's the right thing to do.

This happened with one of our children. A friend's relationship broke up, and the "dumpee" got very depressed. The teen wouldn't eat and started talking regularly about dying. My child asked for advice, and I suggested talking with the teacher. The whole group of friends went to the teacher, one at a time, and expressed their concerns and observations. The teacher handled the matter promptly and discreetly and got the child the needed help.

Another situation would be if your child overheard talk about guns, weapons, or possible violence. Many school systems now have anonymous hotlines so students can report situations like this in confidence. If not, the guidance office is a good place to start. Make the call yourself, if necessary.

Be there to help your children sort out these kinds of situations, because sometimes they're not that cut and dried.

Who's Calling, Please?

Phone etiquette—or the appalling lack thereof—is one of our pet peeves. We constantly pick up the phone only to have the caller ask us who we are. Or someone starts talking without identifying himself or herself. Caller ID is increasingly popular, but don't assume that everyone subscribes to it.

Phone etiquette demands that when you call someone's home, you first tell the person who answers who you are and then ask for the person to whom you'd like to speak. We let our children know we expect the same from their friends when they call our house. If children call our house and won't give their names, they get a warning and then get hung up on the next time it happens. Our children claim that's rude; we maintain not. We should not have to figure out who's calling. Our kids have reluctantly trained their friends and are starting to see the benefits of this system.

We had one case when a young man called our house and Harry answered. "Is Michele there?" the boy asked.

Harry asked, "Who's calling?"

Pause. "Is Michele there?"

Harry again asked the young man to identify himself. Longer pause. "Is Michele there?"

Finally Harry said, "If you don't tell me who you are, you don't get to talk to anyone here." Click. That young man never tried that again. It's perfectly acceptable that we know to whom our children are talking on the phone. If the caller won't give a name, that's too bad. He or she doesn't get to talk to anyone.

Also, teach your kids to speak slowly and clearly when leaving a message. We constantly get garbled messages that are a complete mystery.

These things are all about repetition. Your children will tell you they don't matter, but instill them anyway. Hopefully, by the time they leave home, good manners and polite speech will be second nature to them.

As you instill manners and etiquette in your children, ask yourself:

- Am I respectful in addressing my elders?
- Am I teaching my children to do the same?
- Do we apply the "Thumper" rule in our house?

If you have late elementary/middle school children:

- Have I taught my children how to politely speak up at school when necessary?
- What's the consequence for "being ugly" to people? Do I enforce it?
- Have I instilled in my children the right way to address adults?
- Do my children know proper phone etiquette?

If you have older teens:

- Do I gossip?

- Have I taught my teens to make eye contact and not to mumble?
- Do they know how to speak with store clerks and other adults in restaurants and stores?
- Do they know they can come to me with any problem? Have I told them that?

12

Single-Parent and Blended Families

M y son is my best friend," a single mom told me. "He's everything to me, my reason for living. Everything I do is for him. I just want him to be happy." Given the horrible home situation these two had escaped, part of me understood the fierceness of her protective instincts, but I worried nonetheless. Parents want to shield their children. We want them safe and happy and healthy. But sometimes that desire can inadvertently become too much of a good thing, especially in single-parent families.

This mother and son went everywhere together, shared everything, and became inseparable. She gradually lost touch with her friends and poured more and more of herself into her child. But by the time her son was halfway through high school, the chains of love began to chafe.

The more he tried to pull away and forge his own identity, the tighter she held on.

Thankfully, this single mom realized what was happening before he completely pushed her away. She learned to give him his space and made time for her own interests and friends. It wasn't easy, but she carefully eliminated the best-friends scenario that wasn't working for either of them and reestablished the parent-child boundaries in their mother-son relationship.

As a single parent for several years, I sympathize with this mom. Being both mother and father is no easy task. If you're a single parent, find a support system. And if you know some single parents, become part of their support system.

New Game Plan

After a divorce or the death of a parent (though I'll primarily address divorce situations here), virtually everything changes. The first few months, especially, are an incredibly difficult time of transition for everyone. All the usual rules are different, and nothing looks or feels the same, so family members inevitably flail around searching for equilibrium. Emotions churn like waves, and stress levels rise higher than storm surges. Recognize that finding a new sense of "normal" and grieving the loss of the old one is a process that takes time.

If you have not attended a divorce recovery class, you owe it to yourself and your children to do so. A divorce is devastating for all concerned. How well you handle it and recover from the trauma will have a huge impact on how your children handle it. They need you now more than ever; one of these classes will help you deal with it so you can help them recover too.

Holiday Shuffle

One of the hard adjustments for divorced parents is that holidays are now carefully allocated and divided. You no longer get to spend every holiday with your children, but you must alternate holidays—or portions of holidays—with your former spouse.

This division was incredibly hard for our family to get used to. My children's father lives fifteen hundred miles away. The first Christmas they spent with him, I spent in tears. Fortunately, my friends wouldn't let me sit home alone and cry. They dragged me out and kept me from moping, but it was still tough. Thankfully, I realized self-pity and sniveling weren't good long-term solutions.

After I remarried, my husband, Harry, and I devised a plan that works for our side of the family. We started "early Christmas" in mid-December primarily for those years our kids go north for Christmas break. We've learned that the point isn't the actual date: it's the celebration and togetherness.

When December 24 rolls around, Harry and I alternate between his folks and mine and make sure we call the kids, encouraging—and freeing—them to enjoy this time with their dad's family.

Start New Traditions

Sometimes it helps everyone if you come up with new ways to do familiar things. Sitting around pining for what used to be helps no one, parent or child. Ask your children to share their most important traditions with you. If the tradition just can't continue in the old way, devise a new way to capture its warmth and joy. After my divorce, the kids and I started decorating for Christmas on the day after Thanksgiving so we could enjoy Christmastime to the hilt. More than ten years later, that is still a tradition we value highly.

Summertime Blues

During the summer, most children of divorced parents spend extended time with their noncustodial parent. This can be tough, especially if the children travel far away. When my daughter was three, she said, "Mommy, when I'm with you, I miss Daddy. And when I'm with Daddy, I miss you."

That, of course, is the heart-wrenching reality of divorce. The children can never be with both parents at the same time, not in the way they want to be. If you are considering divorce, think long and hard about the effects on your children.

When the children travel to their other parent's home, try to make the transition as easy on them as possible. Remember that things won't be done the same way you do them. That's OK. Be supportive of your former spouse's rules and standards and, if possible, communicate clearly, parent to parent.

Then keep busy while the children are gone, and do some things for yourself that you normally don't have time to do. The summer can become a time of opportunity, not punishment. Not only does that attitude help you, it keeps your children from worrying about you while they're gone, which is not their job. If they know you'll be OK, it frees them up to enjoy the time away. I do my level best to send my kids off with a smile and save any tears until after the plane takes off. Then, instead of hibernating, Harry and I tackle major home-improvement projects.

We joke that every summer, the food bill goes down, and the phone bill goes up. But that's OK. Regular contact with you is vital for your children. Between email and cheap phone cards, we're in touch several times a week. We encourage our kids to stay in contact with friends here too, because it helps them feel less disconnected and makes the transition easier.

Dual Households

If your former spouse lives locally and your children travel back and forth between households, never act as though all of this is a huge burden on you and your time. Be prompt and communicate clearly. Your children have two parents and deserve to spend time with both of you.

Long-Distance Parenting

Your child may live with your former spouse during the school year and spend summers and breaks with you. The abrupt adjustment to children, or more children, in the house can be a challenge. Laugh a lot, hug a lot, and plug the children into the family routine as quickly as possible. Set limits and require help around the house. This will make the children know they're part of the family, not simply a guest.

When they're not with you, do everything you can to maintain regular, consistent contact. Despite more than ten years and fifteen hundred miles, my kids' father touches base with them every week. He calls, emails, sends cards and letters, and has remained a constant in their lives. That is so important. Your children need that. Do what you must to be sure they get it.

Bad-Mouthing Exes

Bite your tongue, hard, if you must, but never, ever bad-mouth your former spouse in front of your children. If you absolutely must vent, make certain your children can't overhear. Your ex may have been completely awful to you and be an all-around louse, but he or she is still your child's parent. That relationship must be respected.

It is not your job to tell your children the details of your divorce or what a horrible husband or wife this person was. That has nothing to do with the children. (In an abusive situation, the children's safety is priority one. However, even then, in offering explanations, separate the person's poor choices from who he or she is.)

What went wrong in your marriage is not something your children need to know. Let them know that what happened was between the grown-ups and had nothing to do with them. Assure them that you did all you could to work it out but were unable to do so. Tell them the divorce was in no way their fault, and no matter what you and your former spouse may disagree on, you both love them and want what's best for them.

Children idolize their parents, which is normal and natural. If your former spouse regularly breaks promises or ignores your children, they will eventually see that. It is not your job to point it out. Your children won't believe you anyway.

Protect your children's relationship with their other parent. Don't make excuses, but don't tear down either. Look for ways to support the positives.

Find Outside Mentors

If you have extended family or good friends nearby, especially those of the same sex as your former spouse, encourage them to spend time with your children. I'm so grateful for Harry, who is a fabulous influence on our children. He has never tried to take their father's place in their lives, but he has created his own unique place in their hearts.

Blended House Rules

If you remarry, you and your new spouse need to set up house rules right from the get-go. If possible, move to a new place so everyone starts fresh, without territorial issues to overcome. The younger the children are when a stepparent arrives on the scene, the easier the transition will be. Older children and teens may harbor resentment, and the adjustment will take time. Be patient. Don't force a relationship, but let your new spouse and the children form their own bond, in their own time.

Discipline can be a tough issue, especially in blended families. Your best shot at family harmony is to make sure the house rules apply equally to everyone: his, mine, ours, and us. This will eliminate cries of unfairness and go a long way toward building family unity.

Moving On

Bitterness and anger toward your former spouse doesn't hurt the other person; it hurts you and your children. To forgive does not mean to accept what the other person did or to say it was OK. To forgive means to choose to let go.

I've met people who are stuck in the muck. Every time I talk to them, they're still voicing the same complaints, fighting the same battles, year after year after year. If you're having trouble moving on, find a good counselor to help you work through it. You—and your children—will be glad you did.

Your children need you to be a parent. Accept the fact—devastating though it may be—that life did not turn out the way it should have or the way you thought it would. Then determine to make things the best they can possibly be for your family. Don't stay stuck. Move on.

Let Kids Be Kids

If you confide in your children, you need to make changes, fast. Join a single-parents group and make new friends. Find other adults to talk to so you can keep the line between parent and child clear. It is so common—and so damaging—for the children of single parents to be the adult's best friends. That's not their job.

Don't put adult responsibilities on your kids' shoulders either. They shouldn't know all the details of your finances and child support—or lack thereof—any more than children in a two-parent household should. Avoid saying things like, "We'd go out to eat more if your father/mother wasn't spending all the child support money on (fill in the blank)."

Protect your children from your anger and frustrations. If you must vent, do it with another adult. Don't make your children feel they have to choose one parent over the other. That's a lose-lose situation.

Put the past behind you and move on, without bitterness or resentment. Start new traditions and make new friends. Do all you can to foster and encourage your former spouse's position in your children's lives. Whatever shape or form your family takes, create a stable, loving, fun-filled home. Someday your children will thank you for it.

As you raise children in a single-parent or blended family, ask yourself:

- Have I dealt with my emotions about the divorce, so I can help my children handle theirs?
- Have I attended a divorce recovery group?
- Do I have adult friends I confide in, rather than my children?
- Am I taking care of myself so I can adequately care for my children?
- Have I started some fun new traditions in our family?

- Am I trying to maintain good communication with my former spouse?
- Am I staying in touch with the children when they're away from me?
- Do I ask for help when I need it?
- Do I respect my former spouse's position in the children's lives?

If you have late elementary/middle school children:

- Have I kept the line clear between my role as the parent and theirs as the children?
- How am I fostering my children's relationship with their other parent?
- Have I helped my children deal with the divorce?
- Do my children have good role models and mentors in their lives?

If you have older teens:

- Am I being too open about my former marriage?
- Am I telling the children too much about our finances?
- Do I bad-mouth my ex on a regular basis?
- Do the rules in our blended family apply equally to all family members?
- Do I avoid putting adult responsibilities on my teen's shoulders?

Epilogue

Roots AND Wings

When I mentioned this project to my aunt Liane Brown, who is also a writer and speaker, she said, "Be sure you include a section about parents preparing *themselves* for the children to leave. When our oldest left for college, I was not prepared. We took him to school, and he walked away without a backward glance. I cried all the way home and for several days afterward. We had unexpected company come to the door, and I told my husband I couldn't come out of our room. That had never happened before, because we love company. But I wasn't prepared. My heart was broken.

"After that I decided I would do things differently with our next child. When our daughter went off to college, I hugged her good-bye, and she said, 'Mom, aren't you even going to cry a little bit?'

"I said, 'We talked about this. You're prepared and so am I.'"

I've talked with several parents who had similar experiences when the first child left home. They were caught totally off guard emotionally, and this kind of change packs a wallop. It is going to hurt when this phase of parenting life is over. It will hurt a lot. But here too, preparation is the key. You know it's coming. It's not only inevitable; it's part of the natural process God designed. Start preparing now.

Marriage Alert

Did you know that the empty-nest years are the most vulnerable for marriages? Parents spend twenty-something years raising children, and then suddenly, those children are gone. If the parents haven't invested in the marriage throughout the years, the foundation may have cracked. Not only will that leave you on shaky ground, but what you model for your children will greatly impact them as well. The best foundation you can give your children is to build and maintain a rock-solid relationship with your spouse.

Children decide how marriages and relationships in a family are supposed to look by watching you. So go out on dates, and make time together a priority. Never, ever build your whole life around your children. They are important, but your marriage must last longer than the parenting years. And if the marriage is healthy, the children will be too.

Remember Whose They Are

Someday God will ask us what we did with the children he entrusted to our care. Did we protect, nurture, and bring them up to follow him? Did we give them a solid foundation on which to build their lives? Did we let go when the time came? For moms, especially, that last part is the most difficult.

Your children will make mistakes, big ones and small ones. Be there. Help them pick up the pieces, and remind them that God offers second chances. Always. Failure is not fatal.

Many years ago, as I was struggling to let my toddlers out of my hands for even a little while, a wise counselor told me, "God loves those children more than you ever could. He has put them into your care for a little while, but he holds them—and you—safely in the palm of his hand. Nothing will ever happen to them without his permission or knowledge."

When things are hard, remember that God is not in heaven wringing his hands. If your children wander away, trust his plan. One mother said, "We trust the mail to come, the lights to go on, and the bank to keep our money. Why is it so hard to trust our loving God with our children?" Pray for your children, every day. God will give us wisdom if we ask him for it.

Learn to Let Go

If your children are currently the sole focus of your life, resolve to remedy that. Immediately. Don't expect your children to meet all your needs for friendship and emotional support. Become a whole person, separate from them. The rewards will be great—for both of you.

They say toddlers step on your toes and teens step on your heart. The transition from child to adult is turbulent, scary, and fraught with danger, but don't give up on being a parent before the job is done. Pray hard. Pray often. Stand firm on the things you know are right and true. Your kids won't admit it, but they need to know that while everything in their lives is changing, you aren't. Be someone they can count on to say what they need to hear, even when they don't want to hear it.

Once they hit high school, your kids will decide they know everything and you know nothing. Don't be shocked. It's part of the process. Mark Twain once said, "When I was a boy of 14, my father was so ignorant I could hardly stand to have the old man around. But when I got to be 21, I was astonished at how much the old man had learned in seven years."

Some of the things you are trying to teach your children will not make sense to them now. Some won't make sense until they have children of their own. Some they may never get. Persevere anyway.

Your parenting won't be perfect; your children won't be either, but parent with purpose. Don't just drift through the years. Be intentional about what you do and how and why you do it. Look down the road to what's coming. You know which questions are ahead; have an answer ready.

I heard a story many years ago that sums up the challenge of parenting. It tells of a mother whose son was born with no arms. This wise mother knew that even though she wanted to be, she would not always be there to help her child. The best thing she could do for him was to teach him to help himself.

One day she handed him a sweater and told him he needed to put it on, all by himself. Her son looked up at her incredulously since he had no arms. She insisted he had to do this.

So he tried. And failed. And tried some more. His frustration grew, and tears rolled down his cheeks. Finally he burst out, "Why won't you help me?"

With tears running down her own cheeks, his mother answered, "Son, I am helping you."

Stand firm and give your kids the love, acceptance, and practical skills they need for life beyond your nest. You'll be glad you did when you see them spread their wings and soar into the future God has planned for them.

Suggested Resources

Chapman, Gary. *The Five Love Languages*. Chicago: Northfield Publishing, 1995.

Chapman, Gary, with Randy Southern. *The World's Easiest Guide to Family Relationships*. Chicago: Northfield Press, 2001.

Crockett, Kent. *I Once Was Blind but Now I Squint*. Chattanooga: AMG Publishers, 2004.

Dobson, Dr. James. *Parenting Isn't for Cowards*. Dallas: Word, 1987.

———. *The Strong-Willed Child*. Wheaton: Tyndale, 1985.

Gelsinger, Pat. *Balancing Your Family, Faith & Work*. Colorado Springs: Cook/Life Journey, 2003.

Grigsby, Connie, and Kent Julian. *How to Get Your Teen to Talk to You*. Sisters, OR: Multnomah, 2002.

Hunt, Mary. *Debt-Proof Living*. Nashville: Broadman & Holman, 1999.

Johnstone, Patrick, and Jason Mandryk. *Operation World*. Cumbria, UK: Paternoster Lifestyle, 2001.

Leman, Dr. Kevin. *Keeping Your Family Strong in a World Gone Wrong*. Wheaton: Living Books, 2002.

Leman, Dr. Kevin, and Kathy Flores Bell. *A Chicken's Guide to Talking Turkey with Your Kids about Sex*. Grand Rapids: Zondervan, 2004.

Lucas, James R. *1001 Ways to Connect with Your Kids*. Kansas City: Quintessential Books, 2003.

Lush, Jean, with Pamela Vredevelt. *Mothers and Sons*. Grand Rapids: Revell, 1988.

McDowell, Josh, and Bob Hostetler. *The New Tolerance*. Wheaton: Tyndale, 1998.

Mealtime Moments series. Colorado Springs: Focus on the Family Publishing, 2000.

Pryor, Austin. *Sound Mind Investing*. Chicago: Moody, 1996.

Rosemond, John. *John Rosemond's Six-Point Plan for Raising Happy, Healthy Children*. Kansas City: Andrews and McMeel, 1989.

Smalley, Gary, and John Trent, Ph.D. *The Two Sides of Love*. Colorado Springs: Focus on the Family Publishing, 1999.

Warren, Rick. *The Purpose-Driven Life*. Grand Rapids: Zondervan, 2002.

Yates, Susan Alexander. *And Then I Had Kids: Encouragement for Mothers of Young Children*. Grand Rapids: Baker, 2002.

Notes

Chapter 1: Dealing with Authority

1. Dr. James Dobson, *The Strong-Willed Child* (Wheaton: Tyndale, 1985), 235.

2. John Rosemond, *John Rosemond's Six-Point Plan for Raising Happy, Healthy Children* (Kansas City: Andrews and McMeel, 1989), 48.

3. Jean Lush with Pamela Vredevelt, *Mothers and Sons* (Grand Rapids: Revell, 1988), 37.

4. Rosemond, *Six-Point Plan*, 43–44.

5. Dobson, *The Strong-Willed Child*, 279.

6. Connie Grigsby and Kent Julian, *How to Get Your Teen to Talk to You* (Sisters, OR: Multnomah, 2002), 86.

7. Dr. James Dobson, *Parenting Isn't for Cowards* (Dallas: Word, 1987), 155.

Chapter 2: Show Me the Money

1. Mary Hunt, *Debt-Proof Living* (Nashville: Broadman & Holman, 1999), 41.

2. Ibid., 43–44.

Chapter 3: Personal Responsibility and Self-Discipline

1. Susan Ratcliffe, ed., *The Little Oxford Dictionary of Quotations* (New York: Oxford University Press, 2001), 406.
2. Lush with Vredevelt, *Mothers and Sons*, 106–7.
3. Grigsby and Julian, *How to Get Your Teen to Talk to You*, 39.

Chapter 4: Chores and Life Skills

1. Lush with Vredevelt, *Mothers and Sons*, 120.

Chapter 5: Values

1. Josh McDowell and Bob Hostetler, *The New Tolerance* (Wheaton: Tyndale, 1998), 20.
2. Ibid., 25.
3. William J. Bennett, "Human Events," in *Mothers and Sons*, by Jean Lush with Pamela Vredevelt, 198.
4. Charles J. Sykes, "Some Rules Kids Won't Learn in School," July 1, 2002, http://www.snopes.com/language/document/liferule.htm.

Chapter 6: Talents, Gifts, Acceptance, and Communication

1. Rosemond, *Six-Point Plan*, 96.
2. Ibid., 100.
3. Gary Chapman, *The Five Love Languages* (Chicago: Northfield Publishing, 1995), 38.

Chapter 7: Spirituality

1. George Barna, *Transforming Children into Spiritual Champions* (Ventura: Regal Books, 2003), 34.
2. Ibid., 41.
3. Grigsby and Julian, *How to Get Your Teen to Talk to You*, 21.

Chapter 8: Guys, Girls, and Hormones

1. Grigsby and Julian, *How to Get Your Teen to Talk to You*, 172.

Chapter 9: Exercise and Health

1. National Center for Chronic Disease Prevention and Health Promotion, "Adolescents and Young Adults Fact Sheet," Physical Activity and Health: A Report of the Surgeon General, November 17, 1999, http://www.cdc.gov/nccdphp/sgr/adoles.htm.

Chapter 10: Melding Home Life with Friend Life

1. Substance Abuse and Mental Health Services Administration, "The Importance of Family Mealtime," September 1, 2003, http://www.family.samhsa.gov/get/mealtime.aspx.

2. Grigsby and Julian, *How to Get Your Teen to Talk to You*, 26.

Connie Neumann writes a parenting column for *Family Times*, a new regional publication. The former editor of *Mom's and Dad's* magazine, she has written dozens of parenting articles, and her work has appeared in *Single-Parent Family*, *Big Apple Parent*, *Charlotte Parent*, *New Hampshire Parenting*, *Space Coast Parent*, and *Western New York Family*. She holds a B.A. from the Moody Bible Institute in Chicago and has worked extensively with teens at her local church. Connie lives in central Florida with her husband and two teenagers. Visit her on the web at www.connieneumann.com.